advancing healthy populations:
the pfizer guide to
careers in public health

A MUST-HAVE GUIDE THAT
PROFILES THE LIFE AND WORK OF
PROFESSIONALS IN PUBLIC HEALTH

Book Editors:
Barbara A. DeBuono, MD, MPH
Senior Medical Director/Group Leader
Public Health, Pfizer Inc.

Hugh Tilson, MD, DrPH
Clinical Professor of Epidemiology and Health Policy,
School of Public Health, University of North Carolina

The Pfizer Career Guide Series Editor:
Salvatore J. Giorgianni, PharmD
Director/Team Leader, External Relations
Pfizer Pharmaceuticals Group, Pfizer Inc.

Advancing Healthy Populations:
The Pfizer Guide to Careers in Public Health
Assistant Editor: Lisa Scipioni, MHS

Other Pfizer Career Guide Publications:
Opportunities to Care:
The Pfizer Guide to Careers in Nursing

Full Preparation:
The Pfizer Guide to Careers in Pharmacy

Embracing Your Practice:
The Pfizer Guide to Careers for Physicians

About the Logo:
This book's logo aims to distinguish public health occupations from others in
health care. The people under the magnifying glass signify the population-based
nature of public health promotion and disease detection.

ISBN 0-9602652-4-4

Printing History:
2002 First Printing
2003 Second Printing

Printed in the United States of America

table of contents

table of contents

acknowledgments

Special appreciation goes to all of the many public health professionals who were willing to put time aside to talk about their daily experiences on the job and the time and skill required to get them where they are today. Through their everyday work and accomplishment, these people are just some of the many professionals currently paving the way for all those entering the profession.

Betty Addison

Myron Allukian, Jr., DDS, MPH

Elizabeth Andrews, MPH, PhD

Stephanie Bailey, MD

Bobbie Berkowitz, PhD, RN, FAAN

Jo Ivey Boufford, MD

Sheila P. Burke, RN, MPA

Thomas Burke, PhD, MPH

James Curran, MD, MPH

Ronald W. Davis, MD, MPH

William Foege, MD, MPH

Claude Earl Fox, MD, MPH

Mindy Fullilove, MD

Helene Gayle, MD, MPH

Kristine M. Gebbie, DrPH, RN

Lawrence O. Gostin, JD, LLD

Fernando A. Guerra, MD, MPH

Alisa Haushalter, MSN, RN, CS

Richard Jackson, MD, MPH

Laura Kramer, PhD

Wayne Lednar, MD, PhD

James LeDuc, PhD

Tanya Cobbs Leslie

JoAnn Lewis, MPH

Charles Mahan, MD

JoAnn E. Manson, MD, DrPH

Dale L. Morse, MD, MS

William Parker

Karen E. Pearson, MS

Janet Porter, PhD

James O. Prochaska, PhD

Patricia Raymond, RN

William Roper, MD, MPH

Rima Rudd, MSPH, ScD

C. Mack Sewell, DrPH, MS

George Strait

Lawrence S. Sturman, MD, PhD

Ken Thorpe, PhD

Kathleen Toomey, MD, MPH

Reed V. Tuckson, MD

Thomas W. Valente, PhD

Carol Woltring, MPH

Finally, and most important, the expertise, guidance and everyday support from Hugh Tilson, MD, DrPH, Clinical Professor of Epidemiology and Health Policy, UNCSPH, was instrumental in the development of this book. Thank you.

a letter from pfizer

Dear Student:

Welcome to the world of public health. We are pleased to present this guide to careers in public health and hope to bring to life the myriad roles and responsibilities this dynamic field offers. We aim to help you navigate the breadth of the possible career choices that await you.

Now more than ever the public health profession needs young people to enter the field. That's why my coeditor, Dr. Hugh Tilson, and I are pleased this guide, the first of its kind, has been written for you. As you read these pages, you will come to understand the passion and dedication felt by public health professionals every day. You will see that public health careers are disparate — some careers begin in medicine, others in local public health departments. No matter your own entry point, you will be captivated just like Dr. Tilson and I were when we chose our careers. Most of all, you will sense how every public health professional is committed to "making a difference."

I hope this guide sparks your curiosity and interest and connects you to a career in public health. At Pfizer, life is our life's work. Good luck in finding your life's work in public health. You'll be delighted you did!

Sincerely,

Barbara A. DeBuono, MD

Barbara A. DeBuono, MD, MPH

Barbara DeBuono, MD, MPH, Senior Medical Director/ Group Leader, Public Health, Pfizer Inc.

By Jo Ivey
Boufford, MD,
Dean, Robert F.
Wagner
Graduate
School of
Public Service,
New York
University,
Professor of
Health Policy
and Public
Service, Wagner
School, Clinical
Professor of
Pediatrics, New
York University
Medical School

assuring the health of the public in the 21st century

Welcome to the world of public health — a field that is blossoming and thriving not only in this country but around the world. Public health is a discipline built on an academic tradition of inquiry involving research, teaching and professional practice to prevent disease and promote health in populations. This is in contrast with clinical medicine which focuses on the individual. But public health is more, because the term also refers to the organized efforts of society to assure the conditions for people to be as healthy as they can be.

Jo Ivey Boufford, MD

These efforts involve networks of individuals and organizations in communities which, when working together for health, create a public health system. Until now, the organizations considered most responsible for assuring the health of the public have been the federal, state and local public health agencies. While they also carry a special responsibility for assuring that the public health system functions well, in this new century, these agencies are only one component of a much larger system which includes medical care institutions like hospitals, group practices and community health centers, and community-based nonprofit organizations, private industry, foundations and academia.

The nature of this system is that its organizational components, especially the governmental public health agencies, are nearly invisible to a large percentage of the population. Yet it is only if the agencies do their jobs well and efficiently that citizens in this country can be confident about the purity of the food they eat, the water they drink, and the air they breathe. Public health laboratorians ensure that the blood supply is safe and public health regulatory specialists assure that pharmaceuticals are safe and effective. Public health sanitarians assure that food is safe to eat, that air and water are clean and waste disposal is efficient. When there is a disease outbreak, it is public health epidemiologists who intervene to help identify the problem, while health professionals of every type mobilize the appropriate response.

Often, the disease has been contained long before word of an outbreak hits the newspapers. The irony here is that the less people know of what we do in public health, the better we're doing our jobs.

As you read through this Pfizer career guide, you will see that public health is a tremendously varied, exciting, expansive and dynamic field. Public health requires continuing attention and investment to strengthen its infrastructure at every level, particularly through a continual influx of professionals into occupations both old and new. In the 1950s and 1960s, epidemiology, bio-statistics, and environmental research were occupations on the rise. They were followed in the 1970s and 1980s by community health educators and economists to analyze reimbursement rates and the cost-effectiveness of healthcare. In the 1990s, focus on the fields of clinical and evaluative science and risk analysis increased. Today, some of the most critical of the newer disciplines are communications, informatics and genomics.

Today, we must recruit and train more public health professionals who are knowledgeable in fields related to bioterrorism, and encourage more physicians to become credentialed in public health.

Behavioral and social science research that focuses on health determinants, and social marketing directed towards raising the public's level of alertness and changing unhealthy and even dangerous behaviors, are all emerging as important specialties as the field of public health matures. We need individuals who can look at communities, and how a community's cohesiveness affects people's health or feelings of isolation. There is a sense that the legal frameworks and traditional public health statutes need to be made more uniform — a real opportunity for lawyers. Finally, we should expect more laboratory scientists in public health, and, we hope, more investment in that area.

Since the tragedy of September 11, 2001, we have become a nation and a world on alert. We in public health see this time as an opportunity to raise awareness of our mission among the American public: to protect health, promote healthy behaviors, strengthen community prevention and ensure access to quality health care for all. Governmental public health agencies at the local, state and federal levels provide a critical foundation for the public health system. These three tiers must work together to make available essential public health services in every community to ensure the population's health.

The Essential Public Health Services

1. Monitor health status to identify community health problems

2. Diagnose and investigate health problems and health hazards in the community

3. Inform, educate, and empower people about health issues

4. Mobilize community partnerships to identify and solve health problems

5. Develop policies and plans that support individual and community health efforts

6. Enforce laws and regulations that protect health and ensure safety

7. Link people to needed personal health services and assure the provision of health care when otherwise unavailable

8. Assure a competent public health and personal health care workforce

9. Evaluate effectiveness, accessibility, and quality of personal and population-based health services

10. Research for new insights and innovative solutions to health problems

Source: Public Health Function Steering Committee

Local public health professionals, the first tier, are closest to citizens and in the best position to understand their concerns, identify health problems, and define the resources needed to tackle them. They can also help communities hold public officials accountable for the health of their locales. And it is local public health professionals who must be equipped to give community residents the information they need to be intelligent activists when important issues — such as toxic-waste cleanups and infectious disease outbreaks — demand attention.

In many ways, the state health department, the second tier, is the lynchpin of what must become an increasingly integrated national public health system. State health departments have the lead role in assuring the safety of water and the food supply, maintaining information systems to detect health threats and assisting local officials in responding to them. Many state health departments are also expanding their services to include offices of women's health, minority health, special prevention services, primary care and family health, and medical legal services — often in partnership with other segments of the public

and private sectors. As we build a more effective public health system in the United States, the importance of the state health department serving as a link between localities and the federal government has never been greater.

The federal public health agencies, representing the third tier, are located in the Department of Health and Human Services (HHS), and the United States Public Health Service (PHS). Each agency listed below plays a unique role in making national policy, providing information, setting standards for and regulating the quality of services and financing programs for special populations and specific national health problems.

○ Centers for Disease Control and Prevention (CDC) — the "nerve center" agency; provides fast response to health crises in U.S. and abroad.

○ Food and Drug Administration (FDA) — sets standards for pharmaceuticals and blood products, protects food, assures safe medical devices.

○ Substance Abuse Mental Health Services Administration (SAMHSA) — fights substance abuse, promotes mental health.

○ Health Resources Services Administration (HRSA) — supports safety net providers, addresses national health workforce needs, supports programs for vulnerable populations (HIV/AIDS, for example), the medically underserved, and women and children.

- Indian Health Service (IHS) — Provides health care and public health services to the nation's Native American population.

- The National Institutes of Health (NIH) — Lead the nation in biomedical research.

- The Agency for Healthcare Research and Quality (AHRQ) — Conducts important health services research.

We expect that the CDC and its sister agencies — NIH, AHRQ — will carry forward and support research in areas such as disease prevention, vaccine development and the behavioral and social determinants of health. HHS must work with other federal agencies to examine the impact of economic development, education and the environment, among other factors on health.

The Department must also join in supporting a global health agenda to fight epidemics such as HIV/AIDS and working with poorer countries to develop their capacity to deliver health care and protect the health of their people. We are all at risk unless all nations work together to confront epidemics and address the challenges of aging populations, increases in chronic disease and the problems of violence and population dislocation.

Those looking to pursue a career in public health can take many routes into the field. As you read through the pages of this book, you will notice that many of the professionals profiled have had diverse career launching pads and professional lives. While it is increasingly important to have formal training and a degree in public health to optimize your performance, achieving the goal of public health requires many disciplines and individuals with wide-ranging expertise.

As a primary care pediatrician, my introduction to public health concerns was in the South Bronx, where it was clear that problems such as poverty, public safety and education affected children's health as profoundly as childhood diseases. This experience broadened my view of how to promote health within a community, and I became an advocate for the underserved and community health perspective on the public health care delivery system of New York City. When I went to Washington for four and a half years during the Clinton administration, I was officially part of the United States Public Health Service, in the Department of Health and Human Services. For about three years, I served as Chief Operating Officer for the PHS agencies under the Assistant Secretary for Health, and served as Acting Assistant Secretary for six months. As dean of a school of public service, I currently co-chair an Institute of Medicine committee to study the need for the nation to invest attention and resources in our public health system. Our report is entitled "Assuring the Health of the Public in the 21st Century."

There is no better time to be in public health than right now. The future is truly exciting. Knowledge and opportunities in the field are exploding. We know much more today than we knew ten years ago about how to help people live healthier lives and how to develop public policies that promote health. The work of public health professionals has expanded its classic mission to fight infectious disease to now focus as well on chronic disease, mental health issues, terrorist threats, and improved population-based health in the global community.

I see a bright, varied and exciting future both for those coming into the field and those already working within it. Public health professionals must strive for overall population health improvement, a long term goal that will depend on well-funded research, and a well-prepared workforce. I welcome you to this introduction to the world of public health and its corresponding challenges, opportunities and rewards. We hope you will join in this critical effort to build a healthy nation and a healthier world.

Jo Ivey Boufford, MD, is Dean of the Robert F. Wagner Graduate School of Public Service at New York University. She is also Professor of Health Policy and Public Service at the Wagner School, and Clinical Professor of Pediatrics at New York University Medical School. Prior to coming to the Wagner School, Dr. Boufford served as Principal Deputy Assistant Secretary for Health in the U.S. Department of Health and Human Services from November 1993 to January 1997, and as Acting Assistant Secretary from January 1997 to May 1997. While at HHS, she also served as the U.S. representative on the Executive Board of the World Health Organization (WHO).

From May 1991 to September 1993, Dr. Boufford served as Director of the King's Fund College, London, England. Dr. Boufford served as President of the New York City Health and Hospitals Corporation (HHC), the largest municipal hospital system in the United States, from December 1985 until October 1989. She was elected to membership in the Institute of Medicine in 1992 and received an Honorary Doctorate of Science degree from the State University of New York's Downstate Medical Center, Brooklyn, in May of that same year. She received her Bachelor's degree in Psychology magna cum laude from the University of Michigan, and her MD (with distinction) from the University of Michigan Medical School. She is board certified in pediatrics.

the public health disciplines

academic policy advisor

A TRUE TALE

When he attended medical school at the University of Michigan in the late 1960s, James Curran, MD, MPH, was interested in family planning and maternal and child health. After he graduated from medical school, he entered the Public Health Service. "Many newly graduated male physicians went

James Curran, MD, MPH

into the service in one way or another," says Curran. Dr. Curran was given the choice of joining the Air Force or of joining the military commissioned corps in the Public Health Service with the Centers for Disease Control and Prevention (CDC). Choosing the latter, he took a position as a commissioned officer working in the Sexually Transmitted Diseases Control Division in Atlanta. He enjoyed his experience so much that he remained with the CDC at the end of his tour of duty and residency training, rather than returning to clinical medicine.

In 1974, Dr. Curran received his MPH from the Harvard School of Public Health. He then went to Ohio State University to run a sexually transmitted diseases (STD) research project. Eventually he returned to Atlanta in 1978, where he became Chief of the CDC's Sexually Transmitted Diseases Research branch.

In 1981, Dr. Curran and his colleague were researching the efficacy of hepatitis B vaccine in the homosexual community when physicians from across the country started describing unusual cases of *pneumocystis carnii* and *Kaposi's sarcoma* in their patients. These reports heralded the first signs of what would eventually — and quickly — grow into the AIDS epidemic. It was just as those early cases surfaced that Dr. Curran was asked by the CDC to head a three-month task force to investigate the disease.

> "Sound policies should be based upon sound science, and an important part of sound science in public health is founded on outcomes research and health economics."

Academic Policy Advisor Checkpoint

Are you interested in the policy aspects of public health?

Can you visualize the "big picture" and turn issues into what will eventually become health policy?

Are you prepared to put in long hours and wait to see issues transformed into law?

If so, read on

Instead of three months, that assignment lasted 15 years, during which time he was named Associate Director for AIDS at the CDC and established himself as one of the leading experts in the field. During that time, he helped set policies that are still in place today, such as making AIDS reportable in all states and setting limits on who can donate blood. Dr. Curran also helped develop guidelines for testing pregnant women for HIV and offering antiviral therapy to those who tested positive.

In 1995, Dr. Curran was appointed Professor of Epidemiology and Dean of the Rollins School of Public Health at Emory University, where he also directs the Emory Center for AIDS Research.

Profiling the job

Successful delivery of public health rests on a base of sound policy. Legislation, procedural rules, economic issues and other factors create and regulate the public health infrastructure, and health policies emerge and develop from the dynamic interplay of that infrastructure and the forces and people that created it. Among "other factors" are policy decisions made by important non-governmental organizations such as the Red Cross, recommendations of associations such as the AMA, grassroots political advocacy and feedback from hospital administrators. The many avenues for initiating and influencing policy include federal agencies such as the Department of Health and Human Services (HHS), the CDC, the Office of the Surgeon General, and the Food and Drug Administration (FDA). At the state and local level, policy is made in the governor's or mayor's office, state or local health department and in state or local legislative branches. Policy is also made in the private sector through health care and professional organizations.

Professionals trained in health policy and management have many employment options, including positions at governmental health agencies such as the CDC or the National Institutes of Health (NIH), or state and local health departments. They might also work in academic settings, such as university health sciences centers or hospitals, or in the private sector, such as pharmaceutical companies, managed care organizations and other health finance organizations.

Whatever the decision maker's chosen occupational venue, health policy and management professionals must be prepared to make hard decisions about resource allocation. According to Dr. Curran, public health priority setting should be rational and easily understood. "A logical way to prioritize public health issues," Dr. Curran explains, "is to first determine the number of people affected by a problem, the severity of the problem, and our ability to make a difference in number or severity." A health problem that either affects or might affect millions of people will usually take priority over one that affects small numbers, while a problem that causes either mortality or severe disability would take precedence over one that is less severe. One in

which the patient might be cured or the illness prevented would take precedence over a problem in which neither prevention nor cure is feasible, according to Dr. Curran.

"Much of health policy is determined by health outcomes," Dr. Curran says. An example is the relatively new procedure of combining angioplasty with the placement of a stent in a narrowed coronary artery. "In order for that procedure to be covered by health insurance, it must be demonstrated, through large population-based studies, that it is more effective, more successful and more cost effective than plain angioplasty or bypass surgery." In the case of the angioplasty/stent procedure, research has justified insurance coverage.

Another health policy issue under consideration is insurance coverage for mammography in women over 40 versus women over 50. Research outcomes have ignited a policy debate about which diagnostic tests should be covered and in which subsets of patients. "The American Cancer Society, the National Cancer Institute, the American Medical Association or any concerned women's health groups might recommend — or not recommend — such a policy of coverage," says Dr. Curran. "Those recommendations and guidelines would then be researched and considered as a potential Medicare or Medicaid benefit, and/or part of normative benefits by health insurance companies."

While federal policy regulates the disbursement of Medicare funding and hinders the interstate transmission of infectious disease, most public health regulations are developed at the state level. Communicable diseases must be reported to the state health department. State laws set smoking restrictions and requirements for wearing bicycle and motorcycle helmets. Local laws tend to govern such areas as management of substance use and abuse, including provision of clean needles for needle exchange programs. "Some of these issues require balance between social control and individual freedom of choice — or *should*. To some extent social control may restrict unhealthy behaviors, but excessive control tends to drive it underground," says Dr. Curran. He cites drinking and immunizations as examples. "Prohibition made it very difficult to monitor and evaluate alcohol use." When asked about immunization policy, Dr. Curran says, "It was a long time before we could legally keep kids out of school if they weren't immunized. However, such restrictions served the common good, because a single case of measles in a child who comes to class could trigger an epidemic. On the other hand, you don't want to stop kids from going to school if they have religious reasons not to be immunized. It is a balance, but that's how policies are made."

An AIDS story

The year was 1981. Dr. Curran was at the CDC when AIDS was first described. "In retrospect," he says, "perhaps the most important actions we took at the time were to define AIDS, name it and do methodical surveillance for it. We did all this in the face of conditions never seen before." The case definition of AIDS and the attention to making it reportable to all state health departments, and ultimately to the CDC, led to exceptional early tracking of the epidemic. "We developed and implemented in the United States perhaps the best surveillance system for an infectious disease. In fact, that same case definition and the same surveillance mechanism were utilized throughout the world."

After the initial cases of AIDS were reported in homosexual men, case reports started coming in of AIDS occurring in persons with hemophilia.[2] By 1983, Dr. Curran and the others who were working with him quickly recommended that people who had been found to be at risk of AIDS refrain from donating blood and avoid having multiple sexual partners. They also recommended that people with AIDS avoid having sexual contact with others.

What makes the interventions of Dr. Curran and his associates all the more remarkable is that they were done *before* the actual HIV virus was discovered. But, says Dr. Curran, it was essential to move quickly because the pattern of transmission so clearly pointed to an infectious disease as the culprit. Those working on the outbreak were so certain of the completeness of their surveillance and the pattern derived that they felt prevention recommendations were urgently needed before absolute proof existed of the infectious etiology.

AIDS, more than many other health problems, involved the affected community from the beginning. People with HIV or AIDS were on the front lines of policy advocacy. Sometimes they worked closely with people in the government research establishment, often as close advisors. Sometimes they were protesters, he says. Curran believes such community involvement is a very important part of public policy development.

AIDS policy evolved and did not stop with methods aimed at the original infected core population. Landmark studies in the early '90s demonstrated that medications given to a mother during pregnancy and birth, and to the baby immediately following birth, could greatly reduce the transmission rates of HIV from mother to newborn. At the state and local levels, those critical research results translated quickly into policy for HIV testing of pregnant women and newborns, and into offering immediate antiviral therapy to those found to be HIV-infected. As a result, mother-to-infant transmission has been greatly reduced. "But there is always more work to do," says Curran.

A day in the life
A few years ago, Dr. Curran brought his daughter to the office. "It was take-your-daughter-to-work day," he recalls. "I thought it would be fun to show her around and give her a firsthand look at what I did all day." A few days later, she gave her dad a pin she'd bought. "It read, 'When can we have the meeting about the meeting to plan the meeting?'"

Dr. Curran laughs when he tells the story, and admits his daughter's humor isn't without some basis in truth. "My work breaks out into three main areas: university administration, AIDS work, and work with students and colleagues," he says. "That kind of workday will inevitably entail a certain number of meetings."

"People are starting to understand public health; that what affects our health isn't only our physician, pharmacist or our nurse. It involves a far broader look at society."

James Curran, MD, MPH

As one of Emory's nine deans, Dr. Curran is in a position to engage other academic disciplines in the pursuit of public health objectives. "A public health agenda is a great thing to have at a university with a strong health sciences center, because it really leverages our interdisciplinary strength," he notes. "We have very strong ties with the social sciences, with economics, business, nursing, sociology, anthropology and psychology as well as biology, chemistry and medicine. So I spend a lot of time pulling people together at university meetings and scouting opportunities for interdisciplinary collaborations on public health issues." Dr. Curran also sits on many association boards, including Health Care Georgia, the Institute of Medicine Health Sciences Policy Board, two NIH review panels, some CDC boards, AID Atlanta, Jerusalem House, the World Health Organization and the International AIDS Trust.

While he no longer does much direct research, Dr. Curran is involved in coordinating research and recruiting faculty for the Center for AIDS Research at Emory. He also is a member of the Executive Committee for that Center and the Association of Schools of Public Health. "I spend a great deal of time on those public health-related issues that are compatible with the mission of the school," he says. "Because we are a school of public health in what we refer to as the 'public health capital of the world' — the CDC is located in Atlanta — I believe I have both an obligation and an opportunity to get out there and get my hands dirty. If we want our faculty to be involved, then the dean should also be involved."

career at a glance

James Curran, MD, MPH

2000–Present	**Adjunct Professor** Department of Medicine, Emory University School of Medicine
1999–Present	**Affiliate Professor** Department of Family and Community Nursing, Nell Hodgson Woodruff School of Nursing, Emory University
1997–Present	**Director** Emory Center for AIDS Research, Robert W. Woodruff Health Sciences Center, Emory University
1995–Present	**Dean and Professor of Epidemiology** Rollins School of Public Health, Emory University
1995	**Director** Division of HIV/AIDS Prevention, CDC
1992–1995	**Associate Director for HIV/AIDS and Director** Office of HIV/AIDS, CDC
1991–1995	**Assistant Surgeon General** U.S. Public Health Service (USPHS)
1989–1992	**Director** Division of HIV/AIDS, Center for Infectious Diseases, CDC
1988–1992	**Associate Director for HIV/AIDS** Center for Infectious Diseases, CDC
1985–1989	**Director** AIDS Program, Center for Infectious Diseases, CDC
1984–1985	**Chief** AIDS Branch, Division of Viral Diseases, Center for Infectious Diseases, CDC
1982–1984	**Director** Acquired Immunodeficiency Syndrome (AIDS) Activity, Center for Infectious Diseases, CDC
1978–1982	**Chief** Operational Research Branch, Venereal Disease Control Division, Center for Prevention Services, CDC
1976–1979	**Clinical Assistant Professor** Departments of Preventive and Community Medicine and Medicine, Ohio State University College of Medicine
1975–1978	**Assistant Commissioner of Health for Medical Services** Columbus City Health Department
1975–1978	**Clinical Research Investigator and Coordinator** Operational Research Branch, Venereal Disease Control Division, CDC
1973–1975	**Career Development Training** CDC (USPHS)
1971–1973	**Clinical Research Investigator** Venereal Disease Branch, CDC

1 http://www.apha.org/legislative/wrapup_2001.htm
2 http://uhavax.hartford.edu/bugl/rise.htm

**Legislative
Policy Advisor
Checkpoint**

Are you
interested in
politics?

Can you appre-
ciate the impact
legislation has
on the delivery
of health care
to the public?

Would you
enjoy working
with a varied
group of
constituents
and lobbyists?

If so, read on

A TRUE TALE

Even when she was on Capitol Hill as Chief of Staff to former Senate
Majority Leader Bob Dole from 1986 to 1996, Sheila Burke, RN, MPA,
says she never forgot her original career as
a nurse. "Did I consider myself a public
health professional? Absolutely, but not in
the traditional sense. I certainly believe I had
an impact on public health issues."

Sheila P. Burke, RN, MPA

Early in her career, Burke worked as a staff
nurse in Berkeley, California, but left to
work for the National Student Nurses'
Association (NSNA) in New York. She was
hired in 1977 by Senator Bob Dole to be his
legislative assistant for health care. "I was a
Democrat," she says, "but I thought it
would be a challenge for me. He wanted
someone with experience in health care and
I fit the bill." Burke came to the attention of Senator Dole through the
recommendations of some congressional staff members who knew her
through her NSNA work.

At the time, Dole was a junior member of the Senate Finance Committee,
but he became the ranking Republican on the Committee within six months,
and finally the Committee's Chairman. Burke was Dole's senior health staff
member, and then his Deputy Staff Director. When Senator Dole became
Majority Leader, Burke moved to
the Leader's Office as Deputy Chief
of Staff and then, finally, Chief of
Staff. She says her progression was,
in part, a reflection of his career.

"Making policy can easily
throw you into a crisis-like
environment with a great
deal of tension, but there's a
feeling of enormous satisfac-
tion, of making a difference,
when you find a solution to a
very complicated problem."

When Dole lost the 1996 presidential
election, Burke left the realm of
politics and governance to become
Executive Dean and Lecturer in
Public Policy at the Kennedy School
of Government at Harvard University. Currently she is the Smithsonian's
Undersecretary for American Museums and National Programs.

Profiling the job

The person who enjoys legislative staff work related to health care, Burke says, is someone who is fascinated by both the rough-and-tumble of politics *and* who appreciates deeply the impact legislation can have on the public health, including the health care delivery system's public health services. A legislative assistant on Capitol Hill helps members understand critical issues arising in her field of expertise, and provides useful information to legislators to help them understand their constituents' concerns. Some assistants also help draft legislation. As a specialist in health care policy, Burke's role was to thoroughly investigate specific public health care issues and provide an analysis of alternative points of view. In this role, Burke had an impact on broad U.S. health care policy.

What are the routes into the rarefied field of health care policymaking on Capitol Hill? Some suggest the best preparation includes the practical and legal skills obtained in law school. However, while many lawyers are excellent analysts and articulators of arcane matters of law, senators and representatives seldom choose their staff by consulting the personnel registries of law firms, according to Burke. Others suggest beginning with a university program in public policy or public administration. Burke herself holds a master's in public administration, which, she affirms, helped provide knowledge and understanding of how an organization works and the skills necessary to analyze and develop practical solutions to address its problems. All these skills are useful, says Burke, from formal schooling in law to an MPA to political science, but there is no single set of preparation or credential requirements for the job of legislative staff member. "It is one of the last American bastions of a feudal system of patronage, but one injected with a healthy dose of meritocracy. A member of Congress decides what she or he is interested in and hires you. You can be anything from an undergraduate to someone who has a doctoral degree."

Although Burke's background in health care was the specific asset Senator Dole sought in recruiting her, she considers her general training as a nurse great preparation for her work on Capitol Hill. So many basic nursing skills turned out to be transferable to policymaking in Washington, D.C., she says. "All of the skills that we learn in a variety of life settings are useful here. Nurses are trained to be quick on their feet, strategize, build consensus, solve problems and put together case summaries. Every last one of these skills is applicable to legislative staff work on Capitol Hill," says Burke.

"Through all those years on Capitol Hill, I never forgot my original career as a nurse."

Sheila Burke, RN, MPA

As Senator Dole's Chief of Staff, Burke had the managerial responsibility of overseeing the office and assuring that all staff performed well. "My responsibility with respect to health policy took on special relevance from my having been the Senator's health policy advisor. In the latter position I brought to his attention important issues not necessarily pressing to a Senator's wide agenda, drafted position papers for him once he had articulated to me his broad policy objectives, worked on his speeches, did analysis and directed staff members who were involved. The responsibilities were a broad array of what you might expect for any staff person who is preparing a Member for an issue."

In areas of health care, legislation might deal with issues of quality, cost, financing, safety or ethics. Two laws Burke saw through to passage were concerned with hemophiliacs and hospice care. The first had to do with funding the needs of hemophiliacs. In the past, Medicare had covered the administration of a self-clotting factor, but before the new legislation, a patient had to be in a hospital. Senator Dole's office became aware that people were capable of administering to themselves at home. After a lengthy analysis of that particular issue, including a documentation of all the risks, costs and benefits, Senator Dole sponsored the bill, Congress passed the legislation and now Medicare covers self-administration of the drug at home.

The original Medicare law did not cover hospice care, Burke says, largely because the benefit was neither generally available nor well known in the U.S. at the time of Medicare's creation. Allowing someone to choose palliative care as an option, one traditionally not covered under Medicare, was a big issue. There were many concerns about abuse and ethics, issues that always arise in discussions about Medicare benefits, Burke says. She and her staff scrutinized existing state legislation in Connecticut, talked in depth with the Hospice Association of America (HAA), and worked with specialists in the field. They defined the issues, determined how best to finance hospice care and laid out the roles of patients and physicians. In the end, they successfully concluded a complicated policymaking process, and the federal government now covers hospice benefits under Medicare.

A day in the life

No two days are the same on Capitol Hill, says Sheila Burke — except that on all days, the work of a legislative staff member could easily have broad implications for the U.S. population "and every day is exciting."

Also unpredictable, she adds. Legislative staff workers have little or no control over their agendas, "since the day's activities are generally dictated by

whatever crisis arises, the priorities set by the Congressional leadership and the position the staff member occupies in the office hierarchy." An ability to multitask and shift gears quickly — and to flourish in a fast-changing environment — is essential.

As a high-level key staffer working for Senator Dole when he was a member of the Finance Committee, Burke recalls, she dealt with a wide

variety of issues, programs and initiatives, many with direct implications for the everyday health of virtually every American. These included the Federal Maternal and Child Health program, as well as Medicare financing and Medicaid funding. During Senator Dole's tenure as Majority Leader, she recalls, "I was always at the mercy of whatever was occurring on the Senate floor."

The work of a Congressional staff member is by definition collaborative and team-oriented, with much of the most productive work taking place via meetings, conferences and informal discussions. Burke met often with Senator Dole to brief him on public health issues and help him gain a clear understanding of his constituents' concerns. She also served as a liaison to other staff members, gathering information and views to be digested and transmitted to the Senator. Often, this meant presenting divergent views on a controversial issue, making sure Dole had sufficient information to address the situation credibly and intelligently.

"Washington plays an enormous role in health care, in its financing and structure, and as a result, there are numerous opportunities for legislation to be drafted for everything from the creation of new Medicare programs to

Did you know? According to the National Conference of State Legislatures, health care issues made up a greater proportion of bills in state legislatures than any other topic in 1999.[1]

elder care to the control and regulation of drugs and medical devices," says Burke. "There is no aspect of health care in which the federal government does not play a role, and the daily work of Hill staffers reflects that diversity."

Importantly, Burke's contacts weren't limited to Capitol Hill. Her investigations of key issues — hospice care, hemophilia treatments, AIDS research and others — brought her into regular contact with outside health care experts in many different disciplines. The logistics, strategies and coalitions developed through these interactions were the basis for network building and a great deal of legislation.

>>>> # career at a glance

Sheila P. Burke, RN, MPA

2000–Present	**Undersecretary for American Museums and National Programs** Smithsonian Institution
2000–Present	**Adjunct Instructor** Georgetown University Medical Center, Center for Health Policy
1996–2000	**Executive Dean** Lecturer in Public Policy, John F. Kennedy School of Government, Harvard University
1986–1996	**Chief of Staff** Office of the Republican Leader, U.S. Senate
1995	**Secretary** U.S. Senate
1985–1986	**Deputy Chief of Staff** Office of the Majority Leader, U.S. Senate
1982–1984	**Deputy Staff Director** Committee on Finance, U.S. Senate
1979–1982	**Professional Staff Member** Committee on Finance, U.S. Senate
1980–1981	**Research Assistant** Center for Health Policy and Management, John F. Kennedy School of Government, Harvard University
1977–1978	**Legislative Assistant** U.S. Senator Bob Dole
1975–1977	**Staff Nurse/Part Time** Doctor's Hospital
1974–1977	**Director of Program and Field Services** National Student Nurses Association
1973–1974	**Staff Nurse** Alta Bates Hospital

1 http://www.ncpa.org/pi/health/pd012400g.html

A TRUE TALE

Although a college aptitude test helped direct Janet Porter, PhD, to a health management career, she says her parents' examples also played key roles in her choice of a career. "My mother is a nurse and my father was in

Janet Porter, PhD

management. So it was natural that I became interested in hospital administration." Dr. Porter earned both her bachelor's degree and master's in health administration (MHA) from Ohio State University. In 1985, she received an MBA from the University of Minnesota. "It was only on completion of all three degrees," says Dr. Porter "that I was satisfied that I had a set of tools powerful and versatile enough to tackle a career in health administration — in any setting."

In 1988, Dr. Porter joined the Children's Hospital of Columbus, Ohio, as its Chief Operating Officer, a position she held for 10 years. According to Dr. Porter, that position exemplified one of the many ways hospitals work under the public health umbrella, often in concert with local health departments. During that time she earned a PhD in Health Policy, Research and Administration. After several more career moves, she took a position in 2000 as Associate Dean of Executive Education at the University of North Carolina School of Public Health (UNCSPH). "There are times when I miss hospital work," says Dr. Porter, "and especially working with children. But I do love my current work."

A major component of her job as Associate Dean is new business development, which includes bringing large projects to the school directed towards developing public health managers, leaders and the workforce at large. Dr. Porter marshals the resources for the grants as well. "Our most recent grant involves a feasibility study for a patient safety improvement corps. Prevention of patient injury, through early and appropriate response to evident and potential problems, is the key to patient safety." Dr. Porter also serves as Project Director for the Management Academy for Public Health.

Management Policy Advisor Checkpoint

Do you have an interest in and an understanding of the financial side of health care?

Would you enjoy managing a group of people and developing team rapport?

Do you want to become involved in the work of all departments of your institute, organization, school or company?

If so, read on

Profiling the job

Health administration in the public arena consists of government work at the federal, state or local levels, at the Centers for Disease Control and Prevention (CDC), Food and Drug Administration (FDA), and National Institutes of Health (NIH), and state and municipal health departments. Competent and resourceful administrators are in high demand, especially in the high-pressure world of public hospitals. The private sector includes hospitals as well, group practices and institutions, non-profit associations such as the Red Cross, and pharmaceutical and insurance companies. Some public administrators often work with medical supply companies and with dot-com companies, where, for example, they develop software packages to improve the scheduling of patients in clinics.

Careers in health administration's public sector usually require an MPH. In the private sector, a master's in health administration (MHA) or master's in business administration (MBA) are useful components of any health administrator's educational portfolio. As hospitals, both public and private, have grown in size, merged and become increasingly complex, the curricula in MHA and MBA programs have grown more similar.

Health care administration engenders tremendous responsibilities. Management of human resources, encompassing such duties as determining personnel needs, recruiting, hiring and orienting new hires, is one of the most important responsibilities. "You need to be a coach and encourage your employees to show individual initiative and work together as a team," says Dr. Porter. "It's a task that requires no small degree of interpersonal finesse." Planning and budgeting is another area of central responsibility. Adequate revenue must be maintained, expenses balanced, and staff must have access to the right equipment and supplies in sufficient quantity. All administrators, health or otherwise, must understand how to build and utilize good computer databases of information. While information technology is essential for the running of any business, Dr. Porter says, it is doubly so for the health care field, particularly in hospitals, which rely so heavily on up-to-the-minute laboratory values, patient records, billing and scheduling.

The Management Academy

The Management Academy for Public Health at UNCSPH, a joint project between the School of Public Health and the Kenan-Flagler Business School, is designed to educate public health professionals who have moved into essential management jobs, but have little or no formal management training. "We developed what is called the 'National Demonstration Project' to try to determine if there is a way to take middle managers, public health professionals in their 30s, 40s and 50s, and teach them a series of skills to optimize their effectiveness in public health administration. Our task is to develop significant management skills in 600 people over a three-year time period." The Robert Wood Johnson Foundation, the W. K. Kellogg Foundation, the Department of Health and Human Services (HHS) and the Centers for Disease Control and Prevention sponsor the Academy.

Students at the Academy, most of whom work in public health departments and hospitals around the country, remain in their current jobs, spending the equivalent of 20 days in executive education. The "students" spend five days on the Chapel Hill campus and then return home to do most of their course work through distance learning. They are on campus in August and November and then graduate in May. "We recruit and train them in teams," Dr. Porter says. "They apply as a group, they are selected as a group and they attend as a group." Such team training helps the participants understand the responsibilities of different disciplines and helps them to apply and sustain their management skills back in the workplace.

A day in the life

After she completed graduate school, Janet Porter's first job was with an inner city hospital. "I was the evening administrator, which meant that I was the person in charge from 6:00pm to 2:00am," she recalls. "If a mental health patient had a violent episode and the situation needed to be dealt with, I was in charge. If our laundry supervisor was accused of stealing laundry, I had to handle it. If the ER called to report that a gang member had been shot and the rest of the gang was filling the waiting room, I had to decide what to do." It was a job that required strong managerial instincts,

Did you know?
In a September 2001 study, The Center for Studying Health System Change (HSC) showed that hospital costs accounted for the largest portion of medical cost increases in 2000, at an estimated 43 percent.[1]

Did you know?
In the year
2000 alone,
hospitals
provided
approximately
$21.6 billion
of uncompen-
sated care.[2]

she says, and a willingness to act on the spot — "to say 'this is what we're going to do right now.'"

These days, Dr. Porter isn't ordinarily called upon to make quick life-or-death decisions. But the management skills she honed in her first job have stood her in good stead at UNCSPH, where she divides her time between her duties as Associate Dean and faculty member.

"On any given day, you'll probably find me teaching — my students are candidates for either MPH or MHA degrees or, in some cases, working on a master's in science and public health," she says. "I might also schedule a meeting with a student who needs career counseling or advice on a job offer." Dr. Porter devotes several hours a week to training programs, such as the Management Academy or the Public Health Leadership Institute. "As one of several business plan coaches, I supported the Lenowisco County Health Department in Virginia in the development of a collaborative program to develop a water treatment plan for a former coal camp," says Dr. Porter. "Helping students in this capacity is a very rewarding aspect of my job."

As faculty director of the web-based UNCSPH Certificate Program, she spends time with other faculty colleagues discussing and implementing distance learning courses and curricula. "And, of course, there are the inevitable planning meetings, especially if we're in the middle of writing a grant proposal."

At every stage of her career, Dr. Porter has been energized by the scope and variety of her experiences. "I think one of the best reasons to be in public health management or administration is the range of tasks you do from day to day," she says. "Depending on where they practice, health administrators may have conferences with a city council, hold meetings with disgruntled employees, cooperate with the police, and deliver lectures at speaking engagements." And her current job? "Being an Associate Dean is enormously challenging and stimulating," she says. "And getting to see my students move on to their own careers in public health is a special reward."

career at a glance

Janet Porter, PhD

2000–Present	**Associate Dean** Executive Education, University of North Carolina at Chapel Hill
1998–2000	**Director** Executive Education, University of North Carolina at Chapel Hill
1998–1999	**Interim President and CEO** Association of University Programs in Health Administration (AUPHA), Washington, D.C.
1997	**CEO** Methodist Women's and Children's Hospital, San Antonio, Texas
1988–1997	**Chief Operating Officer** Children's Hospital and Executive Director, Children's Hospital Research Foundation, Columbus, Ohio
1988–1989	**Associate Executive Director** Children's Hospital
1987–1988	**Executive Consultant** The Lash Group, Washington, D.C.
1982–1987	**Instructor and Admissions Coordinator** Graduate Program, Hospital and Health Services Administration, University of Minnesota
1979–1982	**Assistant Executive Director** Children's Hospital, Columbus, Ohio
1977–1979	**Evening Administrator and Director of Government Relations** Saint Mary of Nazareth Medical Center, Chicago, Illinois

1 http://bcbshealthissues.com/issues/healthcarecosts/?PROACTIVE_ID=cecfcccdc9cccecac
2 http://bcbshealthissues.com/issues/healthcarecosts/?PROACTIVE_ID=cecfcccdc9cccecac

A TRUE TALE

Growing up in Santa Fe, New Mexico, C. Mack Sewell, DrPH, MS, was keenly interested in the sciences, particularly the biological sciences and especially the investigation of diseases and their transmission. After graduating from New Mexico State University, he received a master's degree in microbiology from Colorado State University. Dr. Sewell worked for several years as a microbiologist before heading to the University of Texas School of Public Health, where he received a doctorate in public health in 1982. A native New Mexican, Dr. Sewell returned to his home state in 1984 to work as an epidemiologist with the New Mexico State Health and Environment Department in Santa Fe. "I found in the field of epidemiology a way to combine my interests in science, human health, microbiology and infectious diseases into one powerful discipline," says Dr. Sewell,

C. Mack Sewell, DrPH, MS

"That was tremendously appealing to me." He then became State Epidemiologist and Director of the Office of Epidemiology in 1989. "There is a certain thrill about working as an epidemiologist," adds Dr. Sewell. "In this field we are identifying risk factors that can lead to effective interventions *before* the etiology of a disease or condition is fully understood."

Profiling the job

Epidemiology is the most fundamental practice of public health and preventive medicine. The aspects of medical detective work inherent in epidemiologic sciences keep even seasoned practitioners intellectually stimulated. The word derives from *epidemic,* Greek for "upon the people."[1] It is the study of the distribution of diseases, health determinants and disease risk in human populations. Goals are met by testing hypotheses using data garnered from population studies. Epidemiological studies provide the basis for preventive approaches in medicine and public health. Because of the investigative nature of tracking and reporting information, epidemiologists are often called "the disease detectives." The importance of this work, particularly as the world "shrinks" as a result of faster, easier and cheaper air travel and the resulting capability of disease spreading from one far-flung corner of the globe to another in a day, make this an important area for maintaining and protecting public health.

Although most state and even local epidemiologists are generalists, there are various types of subspecialists as well. Some epidemiologists specialize in the investigation of immediate, time-sensitive events such as food-borne or infectious disease outbreaks. Chronic disease epidemiologists study disease states that take years to develop, such as cancer and cardiovascular disease. They investigate disease clusters — a higher than expected incidence of disease in a community. For example, if a Long Island community believed that high-tension electrical wires were a contributing factor to a high incidence of breast cancer among residents, the epidemiologist would investigate the cluster and determine the potential causal link between the occurrence of disease and the exposure.

Other subfields include environmental or occupational epidemiology, which examine and seek to cure problems stemming from conditions of the general physical environment (pollution, climate, etc.) or in the workplace (indoor air quality, ergonomics). "One subspecialty we've developed in our health department is behavioral epidemiology because it is a significant public health issue in this state," says Dr. Sewell. "This specialty includes specific studies around substance abuse, including alcohol, tobacco and abused prescription drugs."

There are different paths to the profession of epidemiology. Probably the shortest, quickest way is for someone with an undergraduate degree to get a master's in public health with a concentration in epidemiology. A second, longer, but popular route is that selected by physicians, nurses and others, such as nutritionists, who may go on to become epidemiologists by earning their master's in public health, either before or after graduation from medical, nursing, or other professional schools. Some individuals earn a doctorate in epidemiology (PhD) or public health (DrPH) with a concentration in epidemiology.

A third means of entry into epidemiology is through the Centers for Disease Control and Prevention (CDC) program called the Epidemic Intelligence Service (EIS). Dr. Alexander Langmuir established the EIS at the CDC in 1951, after he identified the need to train physicians and other scientists to be prepared to deal with biological warfare. Over the past 50 years, the scope of the program has broadened dramatically to teach physicians and other health professionals the applied epidemiological skills needed to investigate infectious disease outbreaks and epidemics. The EIS is a two-year training program that recruits MDs, PhDs and veterinarians, and occasionally nurses, pharmacists and laboratorians as well. Public health professionals, at varying points in their careers, can take part in the EIS program to obtain additional hands-on experience in epidemiology. The EIS recruits spend several weeks in Atlanta in intensive training in the latest developments in epidemiology and biostatistics. They then either remain at one of the CDC Centers in Atlanta, or are detailed out to state health departments or international locations for a field-based epidemiological experience to gain hands-on training working on outbreaks and special projects.

Epidemiology at the state level

The staff of the New Mexico State Department of Health Office of Epidemiology, over 50 people, includes physicians, veterinarians, nurses and PhD and MPH epidemiologists. The staff works in the departmental offices and in the field doing surveillance, investigation, data analysis and evaluation, and frequently interacts with medical providers, data collectors, statisticians, laboratory scientists, program managers and public health policymakers. As the State Epidemiologist, Dr. Sewell says that emergency preparedness is very much a part of his agenda, particularly in these times of easy international travel and threats of biological and chemical terrorism and other public health threats. Such threats include pandemic influenza, large outbreaks of known, re-emerging, or newly emerging agents, or other chemical and environmental threats of natural or manmade origin. "We're making good progress with emergency preparedness," he says. "We've developed our health alert network capabilities so that we can send e-mails to literally thousands of people very, very quickly. We have an emergency broadcast fax as well as an e-mail list that consists of hospitals and emergency rooms, physicians, nurses, hospital-based infection control practitioners and some of our own health department staff."

Dr. Sewell's department is working with both Los Alamos National Laboratory, the Sandia National Laboratory and the University of New Mexico Hospital to improve surveillance in local emergency rooms. They are using a method called *syndromic surveillance,* which examines a collection of symptoms in an attempt to identify a course of illness before lab testing has been completed. The idea is to move quickly from a public health perspective, taking precautions and preparing the necessary treatment measures, before knowing the diagnosis for certain. "Let's say, hypothetically, there was an anthrax spore release. People would show up in the emergency

room with a variety of symptoms and signs but the diagnosis would normally not come until later in the course of their illness. We're improving systems so that this type of bioterrorist-related illness can be identified much more quickly. Better yet, the same systems we are building can help us track some of the other terrors that Mother Nature herself has in store."

Tracking a new hantavirus

In May 1993, the NMDOH received reports that a couple had died within five days of each other from an illness tentatively diagnosed as pneumonic plague, a disease that occasionally occurs in New Mexico. This event occurred in the northwestern part of the state, an area inhabited predominantly by Native Americans. The cases were characterized by fever, myalgia, headache and cough, followed by rapid development of respiratory failure. When they were examined and tested by the state Office of the Medical Investigator's forensic pathologists, the results showed no evidence of plague. Within a week, another physician called the health department to say he had treated patients presenting with symptoms similar to those in the deceased couple. In each of these cases, nothing obvious about the patients' illness, or in some cases their deaths, could be explained. These reports occurred with increasing frequency over a period of two weeks until it became clear an outbreak of some unknown etiology was occurring. "At that point, with 12 dead and no etiology and diagnosis," Dr. Sewell says, "we notified the other regional health departments in the Four Corners region, in Arizona, Colorado and Utah, and called in the CDC."

The CDC team, along with state investigators and the Indian Health Service, collected blood, serum and tissue specimens, conducted exhaustive antibody tests at the state laboratory, performed autopsies, and sent additional specimens to Atlanta. The CDC laboratories ran tests of the New Mexico sera against a variety of known agents from other parts of the world. What they discovered was a hantavirus much like Korean hemorrhagic fever and Puumala virus, the second found primarily in Scandinavia, northern Europe and northern Russia. "It turned out," Dr. Sewell says, "that what we had in New Mexico was a hantavirus that had never been previously described in the United States." There are a number of different hantaviruses and this one was eventually named the *sin-nombre* virus, which is Spanish for "no-name." The original intention had been to name it based on the Four Corners region, because frequently viruses

are named based on a specific geographical location, but no community wanted its name given to the virus. The North American strain produces a disease called "hantavirus pulmonary syndrome."

The New Mexico case brought together the CDC, regional health departments, the Indian Health Service, the University of New Mexico School of Medicine, local and state physicians, epidemiologists and laboratory personnel. The time lapse from the initial recognition of the disease cluster in the laboratory to description of the hantavirus in blood specimens was 21 days. "It was just a really intense sort of operation," Dr. Sewell says. "Compare to that the amount of time it took from the discovery of the initial cluster of Legionnaire's disease at the Legionnaire's convention to the ultimate elucidation of a new bacterial species, which was many months in discovery, and you'll see how extraordinary it was." There are still *sin-nombre* cases each year, although the incidences of new U.S. cases have decreased over the past few years.

A day in the life

When he's not traveling on business or delivering lectures, Dr. Sewell is likely to be found in his office in Santa Fe. While he views himself as "less at the grassroots level" than the field workers he supervises, his work involves daily engagement with the myriad public health issues that face New Mexico. Dr. Sewell's style is clearly hands-on, collaborative and participatory. In his position as State Epidemiologist and the office's head administrator, it couldn't be any other way.

It's 8:00am, and Dr. Sewell is on the phone. At the other end is a field epidemiologist who has been investigating several drug overdose deaths in a small town in northern New Mexico. "Since drug abuse is an important issue to the economic health of the community and thus the state, addressing it is vital," Dr. Sewell later explains. The field epidemiologist is working with the vital records staff and the state Office of the Medical Investigator to ascertain that their data sets and statistics are consistent with one another. But their most challenging task is to go from household to household, knocking on doors and surveying residents about what they know and have experienced about substance abuse in their community.

"Drug abuse is a sensitive issue," Dr. Sewell explains, "and gathering information privately and discreetly is the only way to guarantee that we'll be getting honest answers." A critical mass of accurate and reliable epidemiologic data, he adds, "is essential if we're to craft workable solutions."

Notwithstanding the pivotal role played by field epidemiologists, epidemiologists in the home office in Santa Fe also do much of the department's most critical work. New Mexico's 54 local health offices, which are part of the state public health system, assist with day-to-day surveillance and control of such infectious diseases as *E. coli 0157 H:7*, salmonella and hepatitis, gathering reports from laboratories, physicians, nurses and other sources. Following a recent outbreak of meningococcal meningitis, the state mobilized broad resources to deal with the crisis. Within a two-week period, thousands of individuals were vaccinated, thus minimizing the total number of infections and fatalities. A central factor in the success of the effort was the vigilance, skill and medical detective work of field investigators and state health department personnel in Santa Fe.

Direct communication — by phone or in person — with field and home office staff figures importantly in Dr. Sewell's workday. Maintaining close contact with field-level epidemiologists and applying their findings to the task of protecting the public health is as exciting and demanding as work in any major intelligence organization, he says. At the same time, he often joins staff in intensive brainstorming sessions aimed at analyzing pressing health issues, especially those involving infectious and chronic disease concerns, as well as top-level policy concerns.

"The strongest lure of this field lies in the opportunity it presents to the epidemiologist to influence government policy, and how we, as a society, deal with illness and conditions that affect the health of populations."

C. Mack Sewell, DrPH, MS

Staying in touch outside the office is just as critical, he adds. As State Epidemiologist, Dr. Sewell is responsible for interpreting field reports and communicating their significance to key government decision makers. "It's a matter of assuring that the agency has the necessary resources to accomplish its mission," he says. "Because this is such a poor state, much of our funding comes from the federal level, which means frequent contact with the guardians of the treasury."

>>> # career at a glance

C. Mack Sewell, DrPH, MS

1989–Present	**State Epidemiologist** Office of Epidemiology, Public Health Division, New Mexico Department of Health
1987–1989	**Deputy State Epidemiologist** Office of Epidemiology, New Mexico Health and Environment Department
1984–1987	**Epidemiologist** New Mexico Health and Environment Department
1979–1984	**Hospital Epidemiologist** Veterans Administration Medical Center, Albuquerque, New Mexico
1978–1979	**Microbiologist** Hermann Hospital, Houston, Texas
1976–1977	**Section Chief Microbiologist** New Mexico Medical Reference Laboratory
1974–1975	**Microbiologist** Colorado Department of Agriculture
1973–1974	**Microbiologist** Colorado Department of Health

1 http://witn.psu.edu/2227/word.html

A TRUE TALE

Throughout her years at medical school, JoAnn Manson, MD, DrPH, expected to become an academic endocrinologist. During her endocrinology

JoAnn E. Manson, MD, DrPH

fellowship, however, she grew increasingly distressed by the advanced state of disease she saw in her diabetic patients, including the high prevalence of cardiovascular risk factors and late stage complications. Dr. Manson became convinced that many of the lifestyle risk factors for diabetes and its cardiovascular complications were preventable.

As a result of that clinical fellowship, and deeply motivated by her mother's death from ovarian cancer, Dr. Manson became passionately interested in women's health and disease prevention. She felt that by pursuing medicine from a public health vantage point, she could make a difference in the lives of many people. She returned to school to develop her background and training in prevention and etiologic research, earning a doctorate in epidemiology from the Harvard School of Public Health.

Dr. Manson entered the field of public health by way of a National Research Service Award Training Grant, and then an Andrew Mellon Fellowship, which enabled her to conduct epidemiology research at the Brigham and Women's Hospital, a nonprofit teaching affiliate of Harvard Medical School. There she developed a research agenda, meeting her public health goals through research grants. At this point, her career in preventive medicine shifted into high gear. She remained at Brigham and Women's Hospital, where she is currently the Chief of the Division of Preventive Medicine, the first woman to be named to that position. She is also a full professor of medicine at Harvard Medical School, and a board-certified

"Epidemiologic research is extremely gratifying because it provides an opportunity for scientific and intellectual stimulation combined with public service."

Research Epidemiologist Checkpoint

Are you willing to spend a great deal of time, perhaps years, working toward a single goal?

Does doing data analysis and interpreting study results appeal to you?

Do you enjoy writing papers and are you willing to write grants?

If so, read on

internist and endocrinologist. Her work advances management of disease through individual research and scholarly pursuits, and in her academic roles she trains future public health practitioners to meet the complex challenges of the 21st Century.

Profiling the job

While once focused almost entirely on infectious diseases, most epidemiologic research focuses more recently on preventing chronic diseases. Improved prevention and treatment strategies are made possible as a particular disease's risk factors and determinants are better understood. For Dr. Manson, the intellectual and scientific challenge of public health epidemiology coupled with public service makes the field "extremely gratifying." Because her research subjects are human, results are directly applicable to human populations and immediately relevant to the field of public health.

Epidemiologic research tends to appeal to people with a strong background in mathematics and biology or medicine. Although a medical degree is not required, a background in biology is very helpful. A successful career generally requires training beyond the formal medical curriculum, although some physicians, pharmacists and nurses can do epidemiologic research without additional training. "I also have a doctorate in public health," Dr. Manson says, "and that has provided me with a stronger background in research methodology and biostatistics. Both medical and public health specialties are integral to sound epidemiologic research. They also provide an important perspective on the links between patient care and population-based public health." The field appeals to highly motivated individuals with an interest in public service, she adds.

The focus of Dr. Manson's research has been in the important and under-studied area of women's health, particularly the roles of lifestyle factors, diet and hormone replacement therapy in the development of cardiovascular disease in women. "In the past, most clinical research — especially most randomized clinical trials — had been conducted among men," she notes. That is all changing now. Until the early '80s, few researchers were looking at the role of prevention, intervention, medications and the treatment of chronic diseases with an eye toward the particular physiologic and sociologic context of women in today's world. When attention was paid to women's health early on, Dr. Manson says, "it was nearly exclusively related to reproductive health."

Recognizing the strong need to provide population-based approaches to the care of women and to overcome the research gap that was compromising women's health care, Dr. Manson decided to dedicate her career to helping remedy this disparity. Fortunately, her timing for this work was just right. Dr. Manson found her feelings echoed by the NIH and elsewhere. Starting in 1986, the NIH began to steadfastly promote more woman-specific research, encouraging investigators to examine both genders whenever possible and analyze results separately by gender. In the few years since then, great strides

have been made in meeting the call for such specialized work and in developing strategies to better care for women's health needs throughout their lives.

In her quest for new data on women's health, often as a Principal Investigator, Dr. Manson has initiated and worked on several landmark studies that continue to influence the daily lives of millions of women throughout the world. Principal Investigators (PIs) develop research proposals/protocols and bear primary responsibility for technical compliance, completion of programmatic work, fiscal stewardship of sponsor funds, data analyses and preparation of publications, and compliance with administrative requirements of a given project.

One of Dr. Manson's significant research efforts was her participation as a co-investigator on the Nurses' Health Study, an ongoing study since 1976. Widely considered the "grandmother of women's health studies," the Nurses' Health Study — so named because registered nurses were the participants selected for study — assesses the roles of dietary and lifestyle factors in the prevention of heart disease, stroke, breast cancer, diabetes and other major illnesses among 120,000 women currently aged 50 to 75. Dr. Manson is the Principal Investigator for the cardiovascular and diabetes components of the study. Her research concentrates not only on lifestyle factors but also on genetic and biochemical predictors of both heart disease and diabetes — predictors such as the inflammatory markers known as C-reactive protein, and gene-environment interactions. She has discovered through her lifestyle-related research that brisk walking is as effective as vigorous exercise in lowering a woman's risk of heart attack.[2] This study drives innumerable public health and clinical approaches to the prevention of disease and care for women worldwide.

Dr. Manson is also a lead investigator of several randomized clinical trials, including the Women's Health Initiative, the largest study of women's health ever undertaken in the United States. The initiative conducts ongoing work at 40 clinical centers around the country; Dr. Manson is Principal Investigator at Brigham and Women's Hospital's Vanguard Clinical Center, in Boston. This study addresses the balance of benefits and risks of hormone replacement therapy. Of the total of 164,000 postmenopausal U.S. women enrolled in the study, nearly 50,000 are asked either to adhere to a diet of no more than 20 percent of calories from fat daily or to continue their usual diet. Another goal is to assess hormone replacement therapy's potential for helping to prevent cardiovascular disease, colon cancer, osteoporosis and cognitive decline.

Dr. Manson also originated a third study. The Women's Antioxidant Cardiovascular Study (WACS) examines important antioxidants (vitamin E, vitamin C, beta-carotene) and the B-complex vitamins (folic acid, B6, B12) to determine their efficacy in preventing cardiovascular events in high-risk women with cardiovascular disease (CVD) or multiple CVD risk factors. As PI, Dr. Manson designed the study, secured funding, and recruited the study population. She then assembled a multidisciplinary team of cardiologists, nutritionists, epidemiologists and biostatisticians, conducted follow-up, obtained medical records for disease endpoints and maintained high levels of compliance by studying subjects undergoing the antioxidant treatment regimens. These studies all flowed from the early experiences of a young physician-fellow who viewed clinical conditions daily from the perspective of population-based epidemiology and public health.

Studies looking into genetic determinants have emerged as an important subspecialty within the field of epidemiological research. These studies have substantial clinical applications, including methods to identify those at increased risk and to replace defective genes. Such work requires a nearly continuous process of education. Dr. Manson says, "Newly trained epidemiologists are really just beginning their education. The nature of epidemiology is such that one's entire professional life is a life of learning."

A day in the life

While Dr. Manson is first and foremost a researcher, she also maintains a clinical practice, spending one day a week seeing endocrinology and primary care clinic patients — mostly female patients with health problems specific to women. It makes for a long day and a challenging schedule, she admits. But the direct contact with patients helps her stay current with the latest developments in clinical medicine and close to the roots of her career path. As a hospital division chief, she also handles administrative duties and teaching. "It can sometimes be difficult to set aside half my time for research, much as I'd like to," she says.

Given the amount of juggling she does, it's not surprising that Dr. Manson's days are tremendously varied. She might start with an early-morning grant-planning meeting, and then join some of her team members, including epidemiologist colleagues, to analyze a database of biomarker predictors of a disease state under investigation. "As a researcher, I put in a lot of time doing data analysis and interpreting study results and planning out the next steps in framing research questions," she says. She tries to save her afternoons for writing papers and grant proposals.

What Dr. Manson enjoys most, however, are teaching and mentoring — "meeting with students and junior faculty to discuss their research projects and trying, if possible, to guide some of their decision-making as they discover their own interests and passions and plan their futures." The flip side of teaching is learning, and Dr. Manson attends seminars whenever possible to expand her knowledge and hone her skills in new areas. Recently, she has been especially interested in molecular genetics.

Dr. Manson is passionate about the subject of public health and continues to make time to teach at both the school of public health and the medical school. She also lectures as a guest in many courses and to community and women's groups around the country.

"Epidemiology is rarely done by an individual alone. It is nearly always a collaborative effort."

JoAnn Manson, MD, DrPH

"Because much of our research impacts women's health in general, I feel it's important to speak to lay audiences as well as to fellow professionals," she says. The audience feedback she receives after these sessions is almost uniformly positive. "As an epidemiologist, I feel I have an opportunity to expand women's understanding of the key health issues affecting them, and this energizes me to stay the course."

It's a mission she takes as seriously as her teaching, research and clinical work. "I've been in speaking situations that went on for four to five hours and left me hoarse for a week," she says. "But if I can make an impact on the health of one woman in the audience — if one case of breast cancer is diagnosed early, or one woman quits smoking or begins exercising — it's time well spent."

>>> career at a glance

JoAnn E. Manson, MD, DrPH

2001–Present	**Professor** Department of Epidemiology, Harvard School of Public Health
1999–Present	**Chief** Division of Preventive Medicine, Brigham and Women's Hospital
1999–Present	**Professor of Medicine** Harvard Medical School
1996–Present	**Physician** Brigham and Women's Hospital
1992–Present	**Director** Endocrinology, Co-Director of Women's Health, Division of Preventive Medicine, Brigham and Women's Hospital
1996–2001	**Associate Professor of Epidemiology**, Harvard School of Public Health
1994–1999	**Associate Professor of Medicine** Harvard Medical School
1989–1996	**Associate Physician** Brigham and Women's Hospital
1991–1994	**Assistant Professor of Medicine** Harvard Medical School
1987–1989	**Instructor in Preventive Medicine and Clinical Epidemiology** Harvard Medical School

1 Personal Communication, Dr. JoAnn Manson, 6/20/02
2 http://www.channing.harvard.edu/nhs/vol7.html#page1

A TRUE TALE

"I was born into public health," says Elizabeth Andrews, MPH, PhD. When she was a child growing up in North Carolina, her father was in charge of milk and food sanitation control for the state. "He was one of those very dedicated old-school public health officials," she says. "We did not go into a restaurant without looking at the sanitation rating, and we never ate anything from the refrigerator without smelling it first." Dr. Andrews has never lost this perspective on protecting the health of a community.

After graduating from the University of North Carolina (UNC), Dr. Andrews attended the UNC School of Public Health (UNCSPH) where she focused on health policy and administration. Her first official job was as health planner for the Secretary of the Department of Human Resources (now the Department of Health and Human Services) in North Carolina. The job entailed conducting needs assessments for health care services for the entire state. It also meant that she would play an important role in the strategic plan for delivery of health care in the state by working with North Carolina's first legislative panel on health maintenance organizations. Her position as health planner was followed by a job at the North Carolina State Health Department, where she ran the state school health program as well as the statewide regionalized perinatal care program.

Elizabeth Andrews, MPH, PhD

As her career advanced, Dr. Andrews realized her interests lay in epidemiology rather than health administration, "because I wanted to be more involved in conducting research and developing more of a specialized focus," she says. When Dr. Andrews heard about an opening in epidemiology at a pharmaceutical company, she immediately applied, and was hired. The work was intellectually challenging, and Dr. Andrews relished the opportunity to work with so many bright, capable people who were leaders in their field. While on the job, she earned her PhD in epidemiology.

Pharmaco-epidemiologist Checkpoint

Does applying the principles of epidemiology to pharmaceuticals sound interesting to you?

Are you interested in a scientific career path with a research focus?

Would you enjoy knowing that the results of your research will make a measurable difference to populations of people?

If so, read on

As a series of mergers increased the company's size, scope and complexity, Dr. Andrews' responsibilities also grew. "The pharmaceutical industry provided a fabulous setting for practicing public health epidemiology," she says. Epidemiology can help shape drug development priorities by quantifying unmet medical need, and can help evaluate the safety of products when in general use outside of the structured research setting. Eventually, Dr. Andrews was ready for new challenges and found exactly what she was looking for when she joined RTI International, a global research organization, to head an epidemiology group, and was promoted to Vice President of RTI-Health Solutions.

"I describe epidemiology as 'the language of public health,' because, in this population-based field, we use numbers, rates and measures of associations to describe the impact of risk factors, behaviors, and health care interventions. These are the measures that guide public health priorities and policies."

Profiling the job

Dr. Andrews is a public health research epidemiologist specializing in pharmacoepidemiology. Research epidemiologists work primarily with data collected by field epidemiologists or with secondary databases, such as electronic medical records databases. They monitor trends in diseases, identify etiologic factors, find relationships between exposures and clinical outcomes, model data and design appropriate public health programs. Field epidemiologists work on the front lines of potential and actual epidemic outbreaks. Both occupations are essential to the health of the public and, as might be expected, frequently overlap.

Though public health and private sector research epidemiologists work in largely the same ways, there are still significant differences between the two groups. "In the private sector, we sometimes may have the luxury of more resources, but at the same time the review process is often far more stringent and focused. All in all, however, the process takes less time, because the study usually addresses a practical and often urgent issue," Dr. Andrews says. Her company, RTI International, is a not-for-profit independent institute geared toward the social and health sciences. RTI has conducted health, medical and pharmaceutical research for the government and the private sector for over 40 years. Its multidisciplinary expertise covers all phases of research, from initial study design through publication of study findings. Typical studies conducted by the organization address important issues such as undiagnosed asymptomatic sexually transmitted diseases, evaluation of the safety of antimicrobial therapy for anthrax exposure, measuring the prevalence and correlates of drug abuse in a large, representative sample of the U.S. population, reproductive toxicology studies, preclinical studies and a host of other concerns

As director of Health Solutions — RTI's first large-scale strategic initiative focused on public health research largely for the commercial sector — Dr. Andrews leads a team of epidemiologists, statisticians, pharmacists, health economists, survey researchers and people experienced in market research and business strategy. The team focuses on health outcomes and the population impact of medicines, biologics and medical devices. "We do economic analysis of the value of medicines, help clients study the costs and benefits of therapy and develop systems that assess the value of a pharmaceutical company's product in the marketplace," she says. This work is extremely important to providers, payors and patients as the need to appropriately utilize innovative technologies grows. Studies utilize large databases that resemble the real world of clinical practice. A managed care organization (MCO) claims database, for example, shows all of a patient's medical care claims, including when a patient visits his or her provider or fills a prescription. "We look at the records over time and develop a picture of what happened to that patient. If you do that with all the members of an MCO, which could number in the millions, then you can clearly evaluate a drug's usefulness." By studying large and broad-based data sets, epidemiologists attempt to characterize the long-term outcomes of care and identify key technologies and management strategies to provide better levels of care. "Of course we do this work with information that has been completely de-identified and we never have access to the individual patient or physician's identity," she says. All such research is reviewed by an Institutional Review Board to assure the confidentiality needs of all individuals are appropriately protected.

As a pharmacoepidemiologist, Dr. Andrews concentrates on different aspects of drug therapy in real world settings. She investigates the use and effectiveness of drug therapy in specific populations to help guide better clinical decision-making. These studies span a wide variety of diseases as well as care settings. The impact on public health, including critical conditions such as HIV and other viral infections, cancer, cardiovascular disease, diabetes

Did you know?
The presence of diseases such as AIDS, TB, STDs, and other acute and chronic diseases has created shortages of research epidemiologists.[1]

and hemophilia, is significant. Other RTI studies have focused on other important non-disease-specific areas such as environmental and occupational exposures, including medical radiation, inadequate nutrition, and alcohol and cigarette use.

One of the studies Dr. Andrews' group has recently completed was a naturalistic randomized trial, designed to compare the effectiveness and tolerability of three different antidepressants. In this study, the treatments were random-

ized, but after the initial randomization, the patients received the same care they would have otherwise received. Other naturalistic studies work by following extant treatments of patients rather than working through randomized clinical trials. Dr. Andrews' team often follow patients by telephone interviews. "In these totally naturalistic studies, we don't have the interventional requirements of a clinical trial, such as lab tests and physical examinations at pre-determined intervals. Since these are not randomized, these patients have already been placed on whatever treatments their physicians chose and we study them after the fact," she says. Another current study uses an existing database to evaluate treatment-resistant depression. These studies are important because they describe, in an academically rigorous way, the outcomes of drug treatments under "real world" conditions. This real-world data is increasingly important to health planners, as they augment traditional controlled-clinical trials as a tool for developing strategies to optimize patient care.

RTI-Health Solutions' studies exemplify the many ways in which pharmacists, public health specialists and various other professionals interrelate. "One of our most valued researchers in the growing world of epidemiology is a pharmacist with a PhD in epidemiology," Dr. Andrews says, adding, "It's just a great combination." For example, public health specialists bring research methodology and a population-based perspective to the study, and pharmacists bring a clinical perspective, an understanding of pharmacologic properties of drugs, and knowledge of the practical aspects of how patients receive their medications. Dr. Andrews' faculty appointments at both the school of pharmacy and the school of public health further illuminate the dual nature of pharmacoepidemiology, an exciting career path for a pharmacist who wants to work in public health.

Dr. Andrews speaks of epidemiology as a primarily quantitative discipline that helps health care professionals understand risks and benefits before taking action. "Although my area is largely research," she says, "the specialty encompasses a wide range of proficiencies, including disease knowledge, research design, data analysis, communications skills and the ability to enlist the help of numerous other disciplines for any given study." To succeed in this field, Dr. Andrews says, specialized training and graduate level courses in epidemiologic methods and biostatistics are required. "Having an MPH or PhD in epidemiology is absolutely essential."

A day in the life
At RTI, Dr. Andrews devotes much of her time to planning new projects or troubleshooting existing ones. Each day brings a heady mix of challenges — scientific, strategic and administrative.

She begins one typical morning on a conference call with representatives of a pharmaceutical company concerning a health outcomes study that RTI-Health Solutions has been commissioned to design and implement. "Providing technical advice to clients is one of my chief responsibilities," Dr. Andrews notes. "But I'm also involved in managing RTI's resources in a way that ensures that work gets done on time and on budget."

Never averse to rolling up her sleeves and immersing herself in hard research, Dr. Andrews squeezes in two hours of work on a CDC study examining the safety of antibiotics used for anthrax prophylaxis. "We'll be meeting with the CDC in a few days to work out a plan for collecting data and setting up interviews," she explains. "The interviews themselves begin at the end of the month, so we're on a very rapid turnaround."

Around midmorning, she breaks away from the CDC project to confer with another pharmaceutical company. This time, the conversation is about designing and evaluating the success of methodologies for targeting its drugs at the appropriate recipients and ensuring proper usage. "I find these kinds of consultative assignments especially challenging and rewarding," she says. "Primarily it's because they involve working with a team of experts from many different fields, and getting everyone focused on a specific research question. There's a tremendous amount of intellectual challenge." In this case,

"Doing epidemiology research in a private setting is perfect for me because here, if I have an idea, I can frequently just run with it."

Elizabeth Andrews, MPH, PhD

multiple questions need to be addressed: "What are the side effects of the drug and how can they be assessed? How can we ensure their proper use?"

As an adjunct faculty member of UNC's School of Pharmacy, Dr. Andrews spends her afternoon working with colleagues and several students on potential study designs and discussing several proposed RTI-UNCSPH research collaborations with university faculty members. Back in her office by late afternoon, she meets with RTI-Health Solutions researchers to review data that have been gathered as part of a current study relating to new drugs for a poorly understood gastrointestinal disorder. She finishes her day conferring with RTI colleagues about several new strategic initiatives, as well as general management and finance issues.

"The days can be long and demanding," says Dr. Andrews. "But because they're so varied, and the projects so meaningful, the work is extremely satisfying."

>>> career at a glance

Elizabeth Andrews, MPH, PhD

2001–Present	**Division Director** Epidemiology and Clinical Research, RTI Health Solutions, Research Triangle Park, N.C.
2001–Present	**Vice President** RTI Health Solutions
2001–Present	**Adjunct Associate Professor** University of North Carolina at Chapel Hill, School of Pharmacy
1991–Present	**Adjunct Associate Professor** Epidemiology University of North Carolina at Chapel Hill, School of Public Health
2001	**Vice President** Worldwide Epidemiology, GlaxoSmithKline
1995–2000	**Director** Worldwide Epidemiology, Glaxo Wellcome
1994–1995	**Head** International Department of Epidemiology, Burroughs Wellcome
1993–1994	**Head** Department of Epidemiology, Burroughs Wellcome
1986–1993	**Head** Epidemiology Section, Burroughs Wellcome
1982–1986	**Epidemiologist** Department of Product Surveillance and Epidemiology, Burroughs Wellcome
1981–1982	**Chief** Office of Purchase-of-Care Services, North Carolina Department of Human Resources
1979–1981	**Manager** Statewide Perinatal Care Program, North Carolina Department of Human Resources
1977–1979	**Health Planner** North Carolina Department of Human Resources

1 http://owl.ben.edu/departments/mph/volemp.htm

A TRUE TALE

When Myron Allukian Jr., DDS, MPH, graduated from the University of Pennsylvania Dental School in 1964, he did not know that there was such a field as public health dentistry. That changed when he was serving in the Third Marine Division in Vietnam. In Da Nang, Dr. Allukian was stationed at the Third Marine Division Field hospital, where he provided both medical and dental care to the Marines. "It got brutally hot there by 11:30 in the morning — too hot to treat dental patients," he says, "So we would shut down for the afternoon." On those scorching afternoons, he would travel to the nearby villages and provide free dental care to Vietnamese children living in orphanages. "At the end of the day, the kids would sing a 'thank you' song to us. That response just penetrated me from head to toe," he says. He was so taken by these children's smiles that he decided that population-based health promotion and public health dentistry were his future.

Myron Allukian Jr., DDS, MPH

Public Health Dentist Checkpoint

Are you innovative and creative enough to design dental programs or policies for a diverse society?

Do you find the neglected epidemic of oral diseases challenging?

Would you prefer developing programs for populations, impacting thousands of people, to treating individual patients?

If so, read on

After three years at Harvard's Schools of Dental Medicine and Public Health, Dr. Allukian landed a job at Massachusetts General Hospital, where he led an effort to revamp its dental health program in Charlestown, at the Bunker Hill Health Center. He was charged with taking an old municipal dental program and incorporating it into a newly developing health center.

"This job is exciting, challenging and personally enriching, because you're making a difference in the quality of life for so many people."

Before the sweeping changes Dr. Allukian helped institute, there were perhaps 700 or 800 patient visits a year, he says. At its peak, the new program accommodated some 12,000 patient visits annually. Not long after that accomplishment, he was named Assistant Deputy Commissioner and Director of Community Dental Programs at what was then called the Boston Department of Health and Hospitals. Today, 30 years later, he still holds the position, although his title is now Director of Oral Health, in what is now called the Boston Public Health Commission.

Profiling the job

What makes oral health a high priority in public health is its universal nature. "It's a neglected epidemic," says Dr. Allukian. Almost everyone has had at least one oral disease, such as dental caries, periodontal disease, malocclusions, infections or cancer at some time during his or her life.

As Director of Oral Health for the city of Boston, Dr. Allukian oversees the development of oral health programs, education and policymaking for his "patients" — the more than 600,000 residents of the city.[1] His tasks could range from ensuring the proper fluoridation of Boston's water supply, an undertaking completed in 1978 after an arduous eight-year battle, to setting up local dental programs in geographically, culturally and ethnically defined neighborhoods, to arranging dental care for vulnerable population groups, such as the homeless and people with HIV.

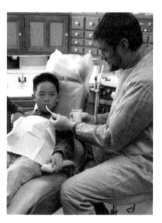

Public health dentists practice at the local, state and federal levels as well as in academic environments. The four major areas of public oral health are: health policy, program management and administration; research; oral health promotion and disease prevention; and delivery systems. Policy work includes such dissimilar concerns as developing dental programs for low-income communities and making recommendations for the state dental practice act.

Epidemiological studies of the causes and distribution of an oral disease would constitute a prime area of engagement for the research-oriented professional. As an example, Dr. Allukian describes research conducted at the Boston University School of Public Health. The primary investigator was an oncologist/epidemiologist. The researcher analyzed the records of individuals diagnosed with oral cancer to identify their health care utilization for the two years prior to their cancer diagnoses. "To our great shock," says Dr. Allukian, "we found a median of nine visits to a health care provider during those two years. How do so many patients — half the sample — have that many visits without anyone picking up that they had oral cancer?" Research conducted in tandem with oncologists is just one possibility for cross-disciplinary cooperation. In the course of their careers, oral health professionals, especially those engaged in research, will probably interact with a representative of just about every occupation in the public health sector. "If we want to conduct a study, we might consult with an epidemiologist or biostatistician in designing it. If we want to create and run a program, particularly in a health center, we need to work closely with administrators and medical clinicians," Dr. Allukian says.

Contrary to popular misconception, Dr. Allukian says fluoridation of the water supply is far from universal in the United States. In fact, more than 100 million Americans do not live in fluoridated communities.[3] "For improvement of oral health for entire communities, fluoridation is the most cost-effective preventive measure at our disposal. Fluoridation costs only about 70 cents per capita, and the measure prevents a tremendous amount of disease,"[4] says Dr. Allukian. Dental sealants applied to the biting surfaces of the teeth is another simple measure to prevent decay, yet 85 percent of 14-year-olds have not had this type of treatment.[5]

When Dr. Allukian became the dental director for Boston in 1970, the city's water was not fluoridated. Dr. Allukian's first steps in getting Boston's water supply fluoridated were to assess the dental needs and to reach out to the community. He did dental surveys and also visited public school assemblies and asked as many as 300 children how many of them had had oral pain or infection in the last week. "Probably a quarter of the kids would raise their hands. Even if I had had 1,000 dentists to treat these kids night and day, we wouldn't make as much of an impact as we could in having the community's water supply fluoridated." He, his staff, assorted specialists, health organizations, and local and state government representatives developed an action plan to fluoridate the water and to persuade Boston's elected officials and those of the neighboring communities of its necessity. After eight long years of this work, all of greater Boston's water was fluoridated, providing health and economic benefits to over two million people.

Dr. Allukian finds his career in the public sector a truly enriching life experience. "In the private-practice sector, I could be making double my income, or more. But nothing can compare to this. At one moment you deal with a person who is homeless or has HIV and cannot get dental care, and minutes later you're talking to the staff of a U.S. senator or the head of a federal agency." The sheer variety of tasks and people is incredibly exciting, he says.

"Let me just say, I can't wait to get to work in the morning and I have trouble leaving at the end of the day. And I've been in this job over 30 years."

Myron Allukian Jr., DDS, MPH

Did you know?
Toothpaste
development
has been
traced to 500
B.C. in the
ancient coun-
tries of China
and India.[6]

A day in the life

Dr. Allukian arrives at his office with "a thousand things to do." He works with legions of public health workers and personnel in different communities to formulate health policy, manage and administer various programs, design research tools, and provide clinical services to patients. As Boston's chief dental officer, Dr. Allukian has a hand in it all.

The first item on today's agenda involves a community-based health center on the verge of shutting down its fiscally strapped dental program. Dr. Allukian spends time reviewing the work completed to date on an analysis of the program's financial situation. "Hopefully, we'll be able to propose a solution that helps staff members improve productivity and get the program on a more solid footing," he says.

Next, he discusses a study with an undergraduate dental student. "She's been looking at a program that is focused on the oral health needs of developmentally disabled children," he says. "We helped her design a study that examines the attitudes and behavior of the child's parents toward oral health. How much knowledge do the parents actually have about oral health and what impact do they have on the oral health of their children?" The objective, he says, "is to see what kinds of intervention we can apply to make sure the children get the dental care they need."

Next, Dr. Allukian turns his attention to a doctoral student who has been evaluating the quality of dental care in four health centers. "Again, the purpose of the study is, ultimately, to identify ways to expand people's knowledge about oral health, and to raise the standard of care," says Dr. Allukian.

Early afternoon finds Dr. Allukian conferring with the advisory committee of a Harvard Medical School program set up to involve more African American dentists in crafting oral health policy. Later that afternoon, he lectures dental students at Boston University. "The object of these lectures is to sensitize dental students to the oral health needs of their patients and the community," he says. "The idea is to get them to focus on dentistry as a calling rather than a business and to respond to the needs of their patients and society on a human level."

Dr. Allukian's days are busy and demanding — and, he admits, "sometimes overwhelming." But what he loves about his work "is that it's extremely exciting and challenging. And the opportunity to make a difference in the lives of people is personally enriching."

career at a glance

Myron Allukian Jr., DDS, MPH

2000–Present	**Director of Oral Health** Boston Public Health Commission
2000–Present	**Assistant Clinical Professor** Health Policy and Health Services Research, Boston University, Goldman School of Dental Medicine
1997–Present	**Adjunct Professor** Health Services, Boston University School of Public Health
1991–Present	**Member** Institute of Medicine, National Academy of Sciences
1977–Present	**Associate Clinical Professor** Oral Health Policy and Epidemiology, Harvard School of Dental Medicine
1970–Present	**Lecturer** Forsyth School for Dental Hygienists
Intermittently	**Lecturer** Schools of Public Health, Harvard University, and the Universities of Michigan and Minnesota
Intermittently	**Lecturer** Boston University, Tufts, and Georgetown Schools of Dental Medicine
1996–2000	**Director** Community Dental Programs, Boston Public Health Commission
1971–1996	**Assistant Deputy Commissioner and Director** Bureau of Community Dental Programs, City of Boston Department of Health and Hospitals
1991–1993	**Assistant Deputy Commissioner and Director** (Oral Health, Homeless Programs and Injury Prevention), Boston Department of Health and Hospitals
1972–1978	**Clinical Instructor** Oral Health Service, Tufts School of Dental Medicine
1971–1977	**Assistant Clinical Professor** Department of Dental Ecology, Harvard School of Dental Medicine
1970–1977	**Chief** Dental Health Service, Bunker Hill Health Center, Massachusetts General Hospital
1970–1972	**Director** Division of Community Dental Health, Boston Department of Health and Hospitals
	Instructor Department of Ecological Dentistry, Harvard School of Dental Medicine
1969–1970	**Associate** Department of Ecological Dentistry, Harvard School of Dental Medicine
1968–1969	**Director** Dental Assistant Training Program (for underemployed women from low income communities), Harvard School of Dental Medicine and Training Center for Comprehensive Care
1967–1968	**Dental Consultant** Curriculum Committee, Training Center for Comprehensive Care, Lemuel Shattuck Hospital
1964–1966	**Lieutenant** U.S. Naval Dental Corps

1 www.cityofboston.gov/residents/default.asp
2 Centers for Disease Control and Prevention, National Center for Chronic Disease Prevention and Health Promotion. www.cdc.gov/nccdphp/oh/flfactcwf2.htm
3 Centers for Disease Control and Prevention, National Center for Chronic Disease Prevention and Health Promotion. www.cdc.gov/nccdphp/oh/flfactcwf2.htm
4 Centers for Disease Control and Prevention, National Center for Chronic Disease Prevention and Health Promotion. www.cdc.gov/nccdphp/oh/flfactcwf2.htm
5 http://www.nidr.nih.gov/news/CONSENSUS/Jane_Weintraub.pdf
6 www.floss.com/origin_of_toothpaste_and_floss

Local Health Officer Checkpoint

Are you innovative in designing programs?

Are you sensitive to the needs of women and children?

Would you enjoy the opportunity to follow a family across generations?

If so, read on

A TRUE TALE

Fernando Guerra, MD, MPH, had just started his residency in pediatrics when he was asked to serve in a unit deployed to Vietnam. "I was a partially trained pediatrician, but overnight I became a surgeon for a combat aviation battalion responsible for organizing the medical support for the air mobile units." Because a considerable part of the U.S. involvement in Vietnam was with the civilian population in villages, Dr. Guerra saw far-advanced cases of plague, tuberculosis, leprosy, hepatitis and many unusual and exotic conditions that, he says, were caused in large part by lack of sanitation and the intense poverty of a country at war. He was also called upon to deliver a number of Vietnamese babies.

Fernando A. Guerra, MD, MPH

His war experience sparked Dr. Guerra's desire to become involved in public health at some point in his career. After his return to the U.S., he completed his pediatric residency and joined the faculty at the University of Texas Medical School in San Antonio. There, he started seeing cases of diphtheria in children. Driven by his concern for underserved communities, Dr. Guerra left academic medicine to go into private practice and established a community and migrant health center in the same underserved area where diphtheria was clustering. The outbreak subsequently turned into an epidemic and, over the course of eighteen months, 161 cases were reported.[1] His commitment deepening, Dr. Guerra realized that if he wanted to pursue a career in public health, additional credentials would be useful. After practicing for almost fifteen years, he applied for and received a Kellogg Fellowship to the Harvard School of Public Health.

"Maternal and child health is one of the most important opportunities open to public health practitioners. In this occupation, one can follow women from childhood through their adolescent, young adult and childbearing years."

A few years after completing his MPH, Dr. Guerra was unexpectedly asked to serve as interim health director for the city of San Antonio. His immediate task was to guide the health department, the city and the Catholic Archdiocese through an upcoming papal visit. The Pope's visit would attract approximately 500,000 visitors, and many public health considerations needed to be addressed in the short weeks remaining. This was Dr. Guerra's introduction to the practice of public health.

After the papal visit, Dr. Guerra was invited to stay on as director, which he agreed to do only if he could also continue to work as a part-time pediatrician. At the end of his day as Director of the San Antonio Metropolitan Heath District, he crosses the street to his pediatric clinic.

Profiling the job

The field of Maternal and Child Health (MCH) "is one of the most important opportunities open to public health practitioners," Dr. Guerra says. "The specialty encompasses the health and well-being of mothers and their infants throughout their developmental stages and over an entire lifespan." Because family structures are intergenerational, important health considerations play out differently within the same household.

MCH is open, but not limited, to participation by physicians, physician assistants, public health nurses, epidemiologists and pharmacists, as well as to those who have earned a general MPH. The personnel needs of MCH range from such highly specialized areas as perinatology and epidemiology to staffing in the most general of all functions, administration. While public health administrators may not be involved in direct patient care, they perform organizing functions essential to MCH programs. Policymakers who allocate resources are especially critical to departments of public health and MCH programs. Family planning, women's health, prenatal services and management of high-risk pregnancy and infertility offer other MCH opportunities. Dr. Guerra suggests that MCH professionals who want to work in the data analysis divisions of public health departments also have credentials in public health.

Programming

Opportunities to design and execute programs that contribute to the health of women and infants at risk are among MCH's most rewarding tasks. "MCH professionals might design a program that helps pregnant women who suffer from the complications of breast cancer, chronic hypertension or ectopic pregnancy deliver a healthy infant. Multiplying such experiences across a community is the essence of public maternal and child health.

Did you know? According to the U.S. Census Bureau's year 2000 statistics, over 23 million children under age six live below the poverty level.[2]

When I joined this department, our infant mortality rate was about 9.2 deaths per thousand births. At the end of last year it was 4.9 per thousand. Many factors contributed to this drop, and good public health practice and our maternal and child health programs were undoubtedly among them."

Practitioners of MCH, to be successful, must employ a multidisciplinary approach to understand and alleviate the problems associated with maternal risk-taking behaviors and lack of access to care. Nurses, health educators, pharmacists, physicians, social workers, epidemiologists and other public health practitioners must work together to create programs to improve access and change behaviors. The nearly halved infant mortality rate within Dr. Guerra's jurisdiction required just such effective multidisciplinary cooperation.

The specialist in MCH is cross-trained to deal not only with women's issues but with children and families as well. At the San Antonio Metropolitan Health Department (SAMHD), two significant programs currently offered are "Healthy Mothers-Healthy Families" and "Healthy Start." Healthy Mothers-Healthy Families aids mothers 21 years of age and younger with three or more children. With the assistance of a Public Health Nurse Case Manager, mothers are taught to create a healthy lifestyle for themselves and their children and to postpone close-interval pregnancies. Healthy Start is a federally funded program designed to decrease infant mortality by bringing high-risk pregnant mothers into the system early and providing prenatal care, case management, education and referral to community resources.

A substantial part of Dr. Guerra's work is attracting support from outside sources to expand programs and services. For example, winning approval of four years of funding for the Healthy Start Initiative will allow the department to add personnel to work in communities at high risk for infant mortality. Even in difficult circumstances, mortality rates can be lowered if a health department builds community coalitions, develops political support and obtains crucial financial support. "We have learned the importance of dealing proactively with high-risk cases and the benefit of improved access to prenatal services," says Dr. Guerra.

A day in the life
A day in the life of an MCH specialist in a city health department varies with training and background. In general, though, the practitioner can expect to spend the day seeing clients at prenatal and well-child clinics, teaching classes

in topics such as diet, family planning and stress management, making home visits, or providing individual and group counseling. "MCH makes for a long day, since many of our services must be offered evenings and weekends to accommodate working women with families," says Dr. Guerra. "But the work is never boring."

Dr. Guerra's responsibilities include administrative work, planning, program development, public relations and frequent lectures. "When you're in a community leadership position," he says, "you have an opportunity to promote immunization programs, flu vaccination campaigns, adolescent pregnancy prevention, adult health screening and other important public health priorities that touch large groups of people."

As a public official with authority throughout the city of San Antonio, Dr. Guerra continually interacts with the mayor and city council, the county judge and the commissioner's court. His actions have an impact not only on the 1.4 million people living in the greater San Antonio area, but on the area's significant military presence as well as several million visitors a year.

"Opportunities to design and run programs that make important health contributions to women and infants at risk are among MCH's greatest rewards."

Fernando Guerra, MD, MPH

career at a glance

Fernando A. Guerra, MD, MPH

2001–Present	**Adjunct Professor** Public Health, Air Force School of Aerospace Medicine
1992–Present	**Clinical Professor** University of Texas Health Science Center, Department of Pediatrics
1987–Present	**Director of Health** San Antonio Metropolitan Health District, University of Texas Health Science Center, Department of Pediatrics
1971–Present	**Pediatric Practitioner**
1980–1992	**Clinical Associate Professor** University of Texas Health Science Center, Department of Pediatrics
1969–1971	**Chief Resident and Instructor** University of Texas Health Science Center
1967–1969	**Pediatric Resident** University of Texas Medical Branch, Galveston
1965–1967	**Flight Surgeon** United States Army Medical Corps
1965–1967	**Dispensary Physician** United States Army Medical Corps

1 Personal communication, Dr. Fernando Guerra, 12/5/01
2 http://www.census.gov/hhes/poverty/poverty00/table5.html

family health
nurse educator

Nurse Educator Checkpoint

Do you enjoy working directly with families?

Would you enjoy consulting and providing a coordination of services for a health department?

Are you interested in improving the health status of a local population of citizens?

Would you enjoy linking families to community resources that enhance their health status?

If so, read on

A TRUE TALE

Patricia Raymond, RN, graduated from Rhode Island College in 1985. Before becoming a public health nurse, she worked in community hospitals and agencies. Eventually, she took a position at the Rhode Island Training

Patricia Raymond, RN

School, the state's only juvenile correction facility, where she supervised and provided health care to incarcerated adolescents. That job taught her to think about population-based health care, and she decided to remain in public health. When a position at the Rhode Island Department of Health became available, Raymond was hired as a public health nurse in Children's Preventive Services in the Division of Family Health.

Profiling the job

Patricia Raymond is a public health nurse as well as the clinical liaison for Children's Preventive Services at the Rhode Island Department of Health (RIDOH). The RIDOH Division of Family Health has five subdivisions: the Adolescent and Young Adult Medical Advisory; Early Intervention Program; Women, Infants, and Children; Immunization for Children; and the Rhode Island Childhood Lead Poisoning Prevention Program. Raymond is active primarily in the Childhood Lead Poisoning Prevention, Immunization and Perinatal Hepatitis B Prevention programs.

Raymond's other responsibilities include conducting surveillance, tracking vaccine-preventable disease and follow-up of vaccine-adverse event reports, and promoting and developing lead screening and immunization programs for children and their families. She conducts classes in the education of health care professionals, school nurses and the public, including parents. Rhode Island has achieved very high rates of childhood vaccination and lead-toxicity testing. Raymond credits her state's continued success to the content of hers and other children's services, adult education classes, and especially to numerous partnerships among health care professionals, community-based organizations and state agencies. Without those collaborations, Raymond says, it would be difficult, if not impossible, to deliver a full range of services.

The Immunization and Lead Poisoning Prevention programs resemble a microcosm of the larger public health department and point out the myriad opportunities for people interested in working in Children's Preventive Health Services. Each program comprises the following members:

○ Program manager

○ Public health advisor — on loan from the Centers for Disease Control and Prevention

○ Vaccine manager

○ Assessment coordinator

○ Epidemiologist

○ Case manager

○ Data quality coordinator

○ Health educator and outreach coordinator

While each of these positions requires its own training, Raymond believes a master's degree in public health is beneficial to any one of them. "I am a registered nurse working on my MPH," she says. "It's not required for me, but the additional education can only enhance my performance in this field."

In July 2000, Rhode Island was honored at the National Immunization Conference for having the second best childhood immunization coverage in the nation, with over 87 percent of the state's children aged 19-35 months appropriately immunized.[3] "To make sure each child is up-to-date on immunizations, we have an assessment team that goes out to the schools, preschools, public and private health care providers and clinics to examine the records. The team enters this information into our database and we provide feedback to physicians on their immunization rates — specifically, which kids are up-to-date and which are lacking."

The Rhode Island childhood lead poison prevention program
More than 100 years after physicians first diagnosed lead poisoning in children, it remains a critical health issue.[4] The federal government banned lead paint in 1977 and the sale of leaded gasoline in 1990, but an inordinate number of potentially lethal lead-painted surfaces still exist in older homes

Did you know?
Although lead paint for interior use was banned in Belgium, France and Austria in 1904[1], the United States did not regulate lead paint use in residences until 1977.[2]

and buildings across the country.[5] Most commonly, children develop lead poisoning from living or playing in such old homes, or where chipped paint leaves a residue of lead dust in the air. Lead can also reside in soil outside or around a house. "The frightening thing about environmental lead is that it is not usually something you can see," she says. "And even more disturbing is the fact that it only takes a very small amount of lead dust to seriously poison a child. The most profoundly sad part of this situation is that childhood lead poisoning — the effects of which are long-term and irreversible — is completely preventable. This is why it is so important to institute and conduct educational programs that will raise awareness in every community across the country."

There are four components to the Rhode Island Children's Lead Poisoning Prevention Program (CLPPP): surveillance and blood workups for all children under age 6; case management of lead-poisoned children; inspections of the homes of children with high blood lead poison levels; and public education and outreach to raise awareness among child care professionals. The goal of the CLPPP is to monitor every Rhode Island child for lead or potential lead poisoning. "First we try to be certain every child has a 'permanent medical home.' That means ensuring the child has a regular physician or managed care organization, or at least access to a clinic where lead screenings are conducted. Children who move to Rhode Island from another state or country, and children who do not have a physician or health insurance, are directed to one of two free clinics," says Raymond. The clinics also make certain the child gets that permanent medical home."

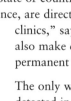

"The most profoundly sad part of this situation is that childhood lead poisoning is completely preventable."

The only way lead poisoning can be detected in-vivo is through the use of blood tests. Without these, a child's poisoning could go unnoticed because the condition is asymptomatic in its early stages. The Centers for Disease Control and Prevention (CDC) has defined the acceptable level of lead concentration in a child's blood as below 10ug/dL.[7] Anything above that level can decrease a child's IQ and may inhibit proper brain development, leaving the child with permanent learning disabilities, behavior problems or emotional and physical disabilities. If the child's lead level registers greater than 10ug/dL, a specific set of steps are taken which follow guidelines set up by the CLPPP. For a level greater than 10 but less than 20 ug/dL, families are provided with lead prevention educational materials and a home visit. Additional testing within three months is recommended to ensure the level is not rising. For a level above 20 ug/dL, the child is referred for medical treatment and evaluation, provided with non-medical case management, and the child's home is referred for environmental inspection to identify hazardous lead wall paint and lead dust in the air.

Currently, Raymond says, educational efforts are focusing on health care providers to ensure that the children they care for are screened according to recommended guidelines. For the parents, the program's educational focus is on augmenting parents' own advocacy skills, and making sure that they talk to their physicians about the dangers of lead.

A day in the life

"A typical day?" says Pat Raymond. "There's really no such thing. "I can be driving to work, mentally listing the things I need to work on, and then wind up getting to none of it that day" Arriving at her office early one morning, Raymond checks her phone and e-mail messages and finds much already on her plate.

A physician has called with a question regarding the state immunization database. A worried parent thinks her child may have been eating lead. A community group wants to book Raymond for a presentation on hepatitis B prevention. And a case of rubella has surfaced in a rural community.

"Rubella is a vaccine-preventable disease and surveillance is a major component of our immunization programs," Raymond says. "When a case is identified, it's reported to me, and I'm responsible for following up and making sure it gets investigated."

As a public health nurse, Raymond participates in various community groups, coalitions and advisory groups such as Healthy Mothers/Healthy Babies, the Head Start Health Advisory Committee and the Rhode Island

"In this type of job, you don't always know what to expect, but I think that's why I like it so much."

Patricia
Raymond, RN

Childhood Immunization Action Coalition, as well as numerous community boards. "Serving on community boards is one of the most effective ways of creating partnerships between the RIDOH and local community organizations and businesses," she says. Partnerships with government agencies, business associations, community groups and others are essential, she adds. "Those partnerships, in turn, become the basis of programs for raising people's awareness of immunization programs, lead poisoning prevention, and other health priorities."

Organizing and conducting training programs and presentations on those and other issues for both health care professionals and parents is another major area of Raymond's focus. "We spend a lot of time on that," she says. "The need for education is constant."

>>> career at a glance

Patricia Raymond, RN

1997–Present	**Public Health Nurse** Rhode Island Department of Health, Division of Family Health, Children's Preventive Services
1989–1997	**Clinic Nurse Coordinator** Rhode Island Training School, Rhode Island Department of Children, Youth and Families

1 http://www.aboutlead.com/history_chronology.html
2 http://www.cdc.gov
3 http://www.health.state.ri.us/family/immunization/home.htm
4 http://www.cdc.gov/nceh/lead/about/about.htm
5 www.cdc.gov
6 http://www.hud.gov/lea/leannual.html#overview
7 http://www.cdc.gov/nceh/lead/factsheets/bllrs.htm#what

THE PUBLIC HEALTH NURSE

For over 100 years, public health nurses have promoted and protected the health of populations, an effort that has taken them from urban apartments to rural farm houses, from quarantined homes to school cafeterias to senior citizen facilities. "The fact that we can practice in so many settings is one reason why public health nursing is so interesting," says Alisa Haushalter, MSN, RN, CS, and Director of Health Promotion, Metropolitan Nashville/Davidson County Health Department. "Another is the interdisciplinary nature of the profession and the many opportunities it presents."

A public health nurse may serve as a staff nurse, a nurse educator, a nurse environmentalist, a nurse clinician or a nurse administrator. He or she can provide immunizations and family planning services in a clinic, make home visits to at-risk families, respond to infectious disease outbreaks, and coordinate emergency shelters for special needs clients in case of a local disaster. While some public health nurses facilitate community coalitions, others might lead education programs on bioterrorism, support groups for children with asthma, or simply provide primary care services. No matter what the task, all public health nurses have in common their focus on prevention, community and the relationship between the two.

Haushalter has come a long way from her beginning in public health nursing. She began her career as a district nurse within an inner city community hospital and went on to develop the nation's first renal case management program and Metropolitan Health Department's first injury prevention program in Nashville, Tennessee. "Public health nursing affords nurses the unique opportunity to work in partnership with a patient in the patient's own community," says Haushalter, who believes that an individual's health is defined within the context of the health of his or her own community. "Public health nursing gives us a frontline view of many of the issues and challenges within our society which can directly impact the health of individuals, families, communities and beyond to larger populations. It's up to us to meet those challenges, and public health nursing gives us the opportunity to do just that."

family health
nutritionist

Nutritionist Checkpoint

Do you understand the physiology of the human body?

Are you well versed in nutritional science?

Would you enjoy working in the community, doing one-on-one consulting and providing lectures and education to children and adults in many venues?

If so, read on

A TRUE TALE

When she was an undergraduate, Karen Pearson, MS, left her home state of South Dakota to spend a summer in Alaska. She fell in love with the state

Karen E. Pearson, MS

and vowed to return one day, "but life intervened, as it always does," she says. After graduating from college with a degree in home economics education, Karen Pearson joined the Peace Corps. She was sent to Jamaica to work in their version of the Cooperative Extension Service (CES), which taught farmers' wives the skills they needed to preserve foods and prepare nutritious meals to enhance the quality of their families' lives. The perspective she gained from this experience had a profound effect, one that changed her career path. "Once I started working in the countryside, it was clear to me the local people needed more than just food planning skills. They also needed basic health and sanitation education, and other basic skills to ensure health," Pearson says.

After her Peace Corps experience, Pearson decided to continue her education and develop a public health focus. After receiving her master's degree in nutrition, Pearson took a job as a nutritionist with the South Dakota Women, Infants, and Children (WIC) program, which provides vouchers for nutritious foods to supplement diets, information on healthy eating and referrals to health care for low-income women, infants and children. Within a year, she was named Director of the WIC Supplemental Food and Nutrition Education Program for the South Dakota Department of Health.

Eighteen years later, Pearson was still in South Dakota, working as the health director for a county health department, when she received a call about an opening in Alaska for the state nutrition director position. "I knew I would go back to Alaska one day," she says. "It took a while, but I finally fulfilled my promise to myself."

As Alaska's state nutritionist, Pearson duplicated much of the important work she had begun in South Dakota. Several years later, Pearson was promoted to section chief for Maternal, Child and Family Health (MCFH) in the Alaska Department of Health and Social Services. She was subsequently appointed Deputy Director for the state's Division of Public Health. In February 2001, Pearson became the Alaska Department of Health's Director of the Division of Public Health in the Department of Health and Social Services. "I think it's great to be able to show nutritionists that they, too, can move up through the system," she says.

"With diverse public health professionals collaborating to enhance a community's health, the nutritionist has a key place at the table."

Profiling the job

Nutrition is public health. The foods individuals consume have a major impact on their health and well-being. Diet and attendant social customs influence the health of communities as well, whether one of pregnant women of a particular ethnic group, or everyone living in a given community. "With diverse public health professionals collaborating to enhance a community's health, the nutritionist has a key place at the table," says Pearson.

The usual image of the nutritionist has been the hospital practitioner, who plans meals and ensures that patients receive their special diets. They comprise only a small segment of the field, says Pearson. Public health nutritionists have the opportunity to work with a wide range of populations, including children with special needs, people suffering from chronic diseases, and the elderly. A nutritionist can educate communities about nutrition, conduct one-on-one counseling or set nutrition policy at the local, state and federal government levels. Universities and private laboratories have an ongoing need for nutritionists as researchers and professors.

Nutrition is an excellent profession for someone who enjoys interacting with people, connects easily with others and believes that sharing knowledge will make a difference. The required skills include an understanding of the sciences of nutrition — digestion, nutritional balance and vitamin needs, among others — and physiology. Psychology, with a focus on how to change behavior and motivate people, is also an important science to the nutritionist.

A registered dietitian (RD) degree is needed to execute therapeutic interventions and to counsel in hospitals and other medical settings. Some dietitians who have large practices in diabetes treatment also become trained and

Did you know?
WIC serves approximately 45 percent of all infants born in the United States and young children under five years of age.[1]

certified as diabetes educators. For most community health positions, a master's degree in public health with an undergraduate degree in nutrition is suggested. If nutritional research is your calling, even more scientific background is required. And if your interest is at the policy level, core public health courses are essential.

At the federal level, nutritionists work at the Centers for Disease Control and Prevention (CDC) to direct programs and research with a nutritional component. They also evaluate grants given to states to examine the treatment of such issues as obesity and physical fitness, and observe the implementation of the nutritional components of these programs. Within the Health Resources and Services Administration (HRSA), nutritionists act as regional consultants to the states, helping to integrate nutrition into programs and to provide technical expertise where needed.

Community nutrition is an important practice area. Women, Infants, and Children (WIC) is an excellent example of a nationwide community nutrition program that employs a huge number of nutritionists to counsel individuals, run programs and set policies geared to populations with special dietary needs. WIC services are available to pregnant women, breastfeeding women and children up to the age of five. Participants in the program must meet specific income requirements, based usually on state poverty levels, and have a nutritional risk. For those who qualify, WIC provides special food vouchers for nutrition-rich foods and infant formula.

The Alaska Department of Health and Social Services develops many programs and has many partnerships directed towards nutrition enhancement. For example, nutrition professionals work with the food stamp program, which entails providing clients with information about making better food choices. Their goal is to make food stamp dollars go further in supplying meals that are more nutritious to recipients.

Nutrition professionals often partner with the department of education to reach children. "There is a very high anemia rate among children in a particular area of Alaska. WIC provides food and nutrition education for children up to five years of age," Pearson says. "After age five, the Department of Education and Early Development (DEED) and the Department of Health and Social Services (DHSS) share the task, and work through the schools to continue supplementing the children's iron intake and educating families, with WIC in a background advisory capacity for the care of the older children."

Obesity in both children and adults, another problem in this country, is a burgeoning area of practice for the public health nutritionist. The public health nutritionist plays a central role in reversing this unhealthy trend,

which leads to many associated disorders, from heart and cardiovascular disease to depression. Through WIC and related programs, and by contributing to changing policy that determines the content of school meals, nutritionists can substantially improve the health of the American populace. "Education and habit-changing are key techniques for the nutritionist. Changing eating behaviors that lead to obesity, such as by acclimating children's tastes to nutritious and low-fat foods when they are very young, is an important strategy in fighting obesity among all Americans, young and old," says Pearson. "After all, children become adults, and carry the habits of childhood into later life, when it is far more difficult to reverse course."

A day in the life

Karen Pearson's title — she is Director of the Division of Public Health in Alaska's health and social services department — does not suggest she is exclusively concerned with nutrition. That her particular background leads to a special understanding of the impact of nutrition on health for individuals, families and communities cannot be denied, however.

"Those in the nutrition field can work at everything from actually being out in the community doing nutrition education and one-on-one counseling to being in a position to establish nutrition policy at the government level," she says. "In all cases, you have a tremendous opportunity to effect lasting change in people's lifestyles and health."

Pearson's responsibilities cover nutrition in the broader context of public health. "Right now we're in the middle of Alaska's legislative sessions, so much of my time goes toward making sure we provide the information

"What and how much people eat have a major impact on their health and well-being, both individually and population-wide, whether the population is one of pregnant women, a particular ethnic group or everyone living in a given community."

Karen Pearson, MS

lawmakers need to support our budget requests and any bills under consideration," she says. Among the bills currently on the table are those relating to funding for nutrition-based programs; others involve teenage smoking, teenage sexual activity, family violence and bioterrorism. "I spend a good deal of time working with other health care organizations and government agencies at both the public health and acute care ends of the system," she

says. "A big part of my job is making sure that we're working together at every level to the best of our ability."

In contrast, one of Pearson's staff nutritionists is likely to have more of an on-the-ground presence in local communities. A case in point: the director of a small WIC clinic in rural Alaska "might start her day on the telephone, referring WIC clients to public health nurses and calling to see if previous referrals were followed up," says Pearson.

But most of the nutritionist's work is live and in-person. "When her phone work is out of the way, she may have several appointments to screen new clients or conduct WIC eligibility recertifications," Pearson says. "At noon, she teaches a class to WIC recipients in healthy cooking methods and the nutrient values of different foods. Perhaps in this class she demonstrates how to cook dried peas and beans and explains their nutritional value."

In the afternoon, the nutritionist visits a high school cafeteria to talk with teenagers about eating disorders. In the evening, she addresses a local community group about obesity and weight loss. "I can tell you from direct experience that a community-based nutritionist's days are long and demanding, but incredibly rewarding," Pearson says. "The day-to-day rigors are more than offset by knowing that you're helping individuals and families change their views of eating and nutrition, and helping them form the foundation of a healthier and, ideally, longer life."

career at a glance <<<

Karen E. Pearson, MS

2001–Present	**Director** Division of Public Health, Alaska Department of Health and Social Services (State Health Official)
1997–2001	**Deputy Director** Division of Public Health, Alaska Department of Health and Social Services
1990–1997	**Section Chief** Alaska Dept. of Health and Social Services, Division of Public Health, Section of Maternal, Child and Family Health
1988–1990	**Chief, Nutrition Services/Health Program Specialist III** Alaska Dept. of Health and Social Services, Division of Public Health, Section of Maternal, Child and Family Health
1987–1988	**Division Director** Pennington County; Division of Public Health and Human Services
1985–1987	**Director, Clinic Services/Special Projects** South Dakota Department of Health; Division of Health Services
1981–1985	**Director, Nutrition Services Program** South Dakota Department of Health; Division of Health Services
1977–1979	**Graduate Administrative Assistant/International Agriculture** South Dakota State University/ACTION
1975–1977	**School Food Service Special Project Director** Child and Adult Nutrition Services/South Dakota Department of Education and Cultural Affairs
1975	**Quality Control Specialist** South Dakota Department of Social Services
1974	**Home Economics Component Training Staff Member** University of the West Indies
1972–1974	**Peace Corps Volunteer** Peace Corps

1 http://www.breastfeeding.org/newsletter/v2i1/page5.html
2 http://www.eatright.org/factsheet.html

health and behavior

By James
Prochaska, PhD,
Director, Cancer
Prevention
Research
Center,
Professor of
Psychology,
University of
Rhode Island

My life's work has been to help people change their behaviors on their own, without psychotherapy. This work began for me after I experienced terrible depression at being unable to help someone overcome the alcoholism that posed a severe threat to his health. Since he refused to seek professional help, it was his loved ones who faced the daunting task of trying to get him to change his behavior. Unfortunately, nothing worked.

James O. Prochaska, PhD

That man was my father. He died when I was a junior in college.

After his death, I began to study psychology in an effort to understand what had happened to him and why he so stubbornly refused help, even though he knew the consequences of his refusal. As time went on, I tirelessly sought a method to help people like my father. I learned in my studies that while there were countless ways to treat troubling behavioral issues, no single approach was adequate for them all. Finding a way to integrate different approaches into a new whole would be my first task.

Once out of school and practicing clinical psychology, I sought a way to bring together the profound insights of psychoanalysis, the techniques of behaviorism and the empathetic relationships of humanism. By combining these with the more common components of major therapies, I thought, I might find a way to treat unhealthy behaviors across the board with a new, integrated approach.

In 1978 my colleague and I devised a model for change that we felt addressed all those issues. Our model — the Transtheoretical Model of Behavioral Change — explores the stages leading to positive change that is maintained over time. It provoked a small revolution in the field, because before our initiative, almost all treatment programs were "action-based," meaning that behavior change was simply a matter of deciding to take action and then moving on that action. For example, someone might say, "I'm going to lose weight." After a period of time, the individual either succeeds or is unable to sustain his or her good intentions. In my experience, most people fall into the latter category.

Through our research, we determined that efforts to change lifestyles achieve greater impact if change is understood as an ongoing process with manageable stages. That understanding led us to develop a multi-stage process that has been applied to all major health risk behaviors, including smoking, alcohol and substance abuse, high-risk sexual behavior, unhealthy diets and sedentary lifestyles, and has dealt with teens, adults and noncompliant patients.

The Transtheoretical Model of Behavioral Change is comprised of six stages: pre-contemplation, contemplation, preparation, action, maintenance and termination. The *pre-contemplation* stage is directed at individuals who are not planning to take action for at least the next six months. That doesn't mean they don't want to change, it means that they know it will take a while to make a firm commitment. These people tend to underestimate how their current behavior affects their health negatively and how much change would benefit them.

Once they progress into *contemplation,* the second stage, they have stated their intention to take action within six months. These individuals appreciate the benefits of change, but they understand that there will be some associated negative aspects. For example, if I intend to lose weight in the next six months, I know I've got to give up some of my favorite foods. I'll have to get through times of deprivation and risk failure, but I'm intending to do it anyway.

In the *preparation* stage, the individual intends to take behavior-changing action within the next month, and he or she has a plan. It may be to talk to a physician, to go to a class or clinic, or to send for self-help materials. These individuals have not started to change their behavior, but are working out the details. It is important in this stage to prepare the patient for a difficult road ahead, and to emphasize the dedication required to get through this predictably difficult time.

Action is the stage at which people actually decide that the time has come to change their behavior. At this point, all of the preceding work we've done with them, especially in stage three, has conditioned them so they have a better chance of reaching the desired endpoint. After about six months of successfully working on behavioral change, the patient progresses into the *maintenance* stage. In this stage, they don't have to work as hard, but they must continue working to keep from relapsing. At this stage we highlight and prepare them for the most common causes of relapse — times of stress, depression, anxiety, boredom, loneliness and anger. Since it is imperative to have a plan to cope with such distress, we suggest three coping strategies that can be quite effective: talking with others about the concern, exercising and learning relaxation methods.

Termination is what we consider the ideal goal, but evidence indicates that not everybody reaches it. Some people must be prepared for a lifetime of maintenance. Those who do reach the sixth and final stage, despite emotional reversals or any other obstacles, have zero temptation to return to their unhealthy behavior. In this stage they are completely rid of the problem, and it is as if they never had the problem in the first place.

After years of seeing this model used in a wealth of different settings and programs, I soon realized it was gaining momentum in public health practice. Public health professionals can modify our model and other models of care in any way that works for them. After all, by effecting change early in populations, it is possible to prevent poor health on a much broader scale. For example, our model was used statewide in a California public health campaign that targeted smokers in the pre-contemplation stage. The results of the campaign were excellent, because the public health professionals running the campaign had tailored it for their target population. The plan implementers didn't ask people in the pre-contemplation stage to set a quitting date in the next month. Instead, messages helped them appreciate the benefits of behavioral change, including the benefits to loved ones of not having to breathe second-hand smoke.

We have conducted stage-matching studies of nonsmoking campaigns that have been tried with various populations in primary care settings, MCOs, in high schools and in walk-in clinics. Smoking cessation clinics, where people just walk in off the street, have usually achieved a very low percentage of smoker participation, even when the program was offered for free. Our method typically achieves about 80 percent smoker participation.

One of the more rewarding aspects of developing a widely accepted method of practice is finding that your colleagues are teaching it to their students. That, at the very least, assures longevity to your work. Our model is currently being taught in advanced behavioral science and communications courses in schools of public health across the country, where students are using it for intervention research and theory and in fieldwork pertaining to health behavior interventions. A psychologist even uses it in a program aimed at helping doctoral students complete their dissertations.

Despite the sad circumstances that led to my entry into the field of psychology, my career has had a remarkably positive impact on my life. It has had a positive impact on many of my patients, and through others who apply my principles, it has led to a broadening of public health models. To know that an idea you conceived and implemented has affected people's behavior in a way that helps them live healthier and perhaps longer lives is extremely satisfying — and to see your life's work implemented all over world, and with such great success, is truly an honor.

James O. Prochaska, PhD, is Director of the Cancer Prevention Research Center and Professor of Psychology at the University of Rhode Island. He received his doctorate in Clinical Psychology from Wayne State University. He has served as a consultant to the American Cancer Society, the Centers for Disease Control and Prevention, managed care organizations, the National Health Service of Great Britain, major corporations and numerous universities and research centers. Dr. Prochaska has won many awards, including the Top Five Most Cited Authors in Psychology from the American Psychology Society and an Honorary Chairmanship of Medicine from the University of Birmingham, England.

behavioral scientist

Do you
want to work
in a field that
directly affects
the health of
individuals as
well as the
health of the
population
as a whole?

Are you
interested in
the causes and
treatments of
addiction and
substance
abuse?

Would you
enjoy creating
programs
designed to
help people
change harmful
behavior?

If so, read on

A TRUE TALE

After his junior year of high school, Ronald Davis, MD, MPH, went to Ecuador for three weeks to take part in a program called *Amigos de las Américas*. In three weeks, he administered 500 measles shots to children in that country, in some cases traveling by mule to desolate regions. That experience piqued Dr. Davis' interest in public health and opened his eyes to an urgent need for more public health care professionals, ultimately leading to his entrance into the Epidemic Intelligence Service (EIS) at the Centers for Disease Control and Prevention (CDC). In the EIS he was assigned to the Division of Immunization, where he worked on the national measles elimination program for two years.

Ronald W. Davis, MD, MPH

In between Ecuador and the CDC in Atlanta, Dr. Davis attended medical school at the University of Chicago. While he was there, the federal government released the first Surgeon General's report on health promotion and disease prevention. At around the same time, a renowned public health professor from UCLA had just described the seven steps to a healthy lifestyle, which included non-smoking, drinking in moderation, getting seven to eight hours of sleep each night and eating regular meals. This made a strong impression on him, and helped crystallize his career helping implement these principles in public health.

Dr. Davis remembers sitting in biochemistry class, having to memorize the eight enzymes of a metabolic pathway and thinking: "What's more important for helping people stay healthy — memorizing a set of enzymes or getting my patients to follow these seven steps to a healthy life?" This way of thinking carried over into his residency in internal medicine at the Michael Reese Hospital on the South Side of Chicago, where many of his patients were obese and had hypertension or diabetes. Again, he thought: "Wouldn't it be better if we could intervene before the conditions developed, by encouraging people to maintain a healthy lifestyle?" With this mission in mind, he went to the CDC, and began his career in the world of public health. During his two years working in the immunization division, he was accepted into the preventive medicine residency program.

Dr. Davis stayed with the CDC for seven years, four of which were spent as Director of its Office on Smoking and Health. From there he became Medical Director of the Michigan Department of Public Health and four years later joined the Detroit-based Henry Ford Health System as Director of the Center for Health Promotion and Disease Prevention. Throughout his career, Dr. Davis has focused on the important work of continuing to prevent poor health by educating people and modifying their propensities towards unhealthy behaviors.

"For someone who wants to make a dent in the toll of death and disease directly linked to human behaviors, it is necessary to understand not only what the behaviors are, but also to be sensitive to the best ways to change them."

Profiling the job

Perhaps half of premature mortality in the U.S. continues to be related to unhealthy behaviors.[1] In fact, six of the ten leading causes of death in the United States are based on behavior, including HIV/AIDS, smoking, violence, accidents (called "injuries" by public health professionals) and substance abuse.[2] Behavioral scientists address these and many other important public health issues through research as well as through work in agencies, hospitals and clinics.

In general, an individual interested in doing behavioral health research first identifies a potentially harmful health-related behavior, and then applies a theoretical model of behavioral science (for example, the Transtheoretical Model of Behavioral Change described in the preceding chapter). Next, he or she would assess attitudes that might be expected to influence the behavior, such as perception of risk, and then design and implement a program which provides methods and strategies for changing the behavior. "For someone who wants to make a dent in reducing the toll of death and disease linked to human behaviors, it is necessary to understand not only what the behaviors are, but also to be sensitive to the best ways to change them," says Dr. Davis.

A clinical behavioral scientist will implement the interventions designed by the research behavioral scientist. As is the case with Dr. Davis, clinical and research work may be done by the same person. For example, programs might focus on child or substance abuse or behavioral changes to prevent unplanned pregnancies and the spread of sexually transmitted diseases (STDs) or tuberculosis. The clinical behavioral scientist will ensure that these programs are responsive to the special needs — socioeconomic, cultural and age-appropriateness — of those with whom he or she is working.

Curbing tobacco use in society has long been one of the leading agenda items for professionals in this field and one of particular interest to Dr. Davis, who for years has been considered a nationally recognized expert in tobacco control. "We have made substantial progress in reducing tobacco use in our society," says Dr. Davis. "The prevalence of cigarette smoking has declined from about 40 percent of all American adults, when the first Surgeon General's report on smoking was released in 1964, to about 25 percent at present." Dr. Davis says there is still a long way to go, particularly with teen smoking. The number of premature deaths caused by smoking still hovers around 400,000 each year in the United States, which is one-fifth of all deaths in this country.[3]

Dr. Davis says that education about tobacco's harmful effects was once the predominant anti-smoking strategy. After some years it became clear that education alone was not enough, and that a cohesive public policy was also needed if tobacco use was to be significantly discouraged. In the mid-1970s, just such public policies began to be implemented in different parts of the country.[4] Policy measures aimed at changing behavior included clean indoor air legislation and laws prohibiting smoking in public places, in the workplace and on airlines.[5] New laws levied higher taxes on tobacco at the federal, state and local levels. Banning of tobacco advertising on television and radio and — through the 1998 Master Settlement Agreement — on billboards, prohibiting the sale of tobacco to minors and state strictures on placement of tobacco vending machines, have all constituted prominent and effective public health policy contributions to the smoking/tobacco use decline in the U.S.

Although Dr. Davis entered the field through a combination of medical training and intensive experience, the field is wide open to any number of specialists in other, related areas. Public health educators and nurses, psychiatrists, psychologists and social workers all can conceivably find bright careers in behavioral science, although, according to Dr. Davis, either the sort of broad and deep experience in the field that he acquired through his career, or formal education in a university behavioral science program, would be necessary. Subspecialties in the field include environment and behavior, natural hazards research, health behavior research and modification, political and economic change, population processes/population aging, problem behavior, the study and prevention of violence and social science data analysis.

A day in the life

Name a behavioral science issue and, chances are, Dr. Davis is involved with it. As Director of the Center for Health Promotion and Disease Prevention of the Henry Ford Health System, he spends his days overseeing an array of exciting programs that encompass the full scope and breadth of behavioral science, from childhood immunization to violence prevention.

A typical day — not that there really is such a thing, he says — might include a review of patients in his smoking cessation program, which is conducted for the center's managed care organization members, as well as a review of health clinics run by the center in eight Detroit schools. In addition, the center administers a community-based violence prevention program, employee wellness activities and flu-shot clinics in companies throughout southeast Michigan. Dr. Davis is also the principal investigator on two large research projects — one examining ways to boost childhood immunization, the other a study of tobacco litigation documents.

The service programs devised under Dr. Davis's supervision are implemented by field-based behavioral scientists, nurses and health educators. "A field worker might spend the day working with residents of a nursing home, employing programs that strengthen their physical and cognitive functions," he says. "In the morning, she might run an exercise program tailored to the special needs of an aging population, with emphasis on optimizing blood circulation. Over lunch, she might hold a roundtable discussion on nutrition and answer diet-related questions from the staff and the residents. Later in the afternoon, she'll engage the residents in a current events workshop."

"As much as 50 percent of premature mortality in the U.S. continues to be related to unhealthy behaviors."

Ronald Davis, MD, MPH

Behavioral research is very much a field-based, on-the-ground activity, Dr. Davis notes. A case in point: A proposed study on the effects of smoking on pregnant women and their babies.

"It's well-known that women who smoke during pregnancy often give birth to underweight babies," he says.[7] "Since premature babies are almost always underweight, a researcher could hypothesize that smoking during pregnancy could also cause women to give birth prematurely." As a first step toward proving that hypothesis, the behavioral scientist will select a suitable community, and then enlist the help of local hospitals, clinics, religious congregations and community groups. Research methods might include door-to-door canvassing, a review of hospital records and interviews with women who have recently given birth.

"The goal is to assemble enough data and a sufficiently large statistical sample to produce a credible — and usable — hypothesis," Dr. Davis says. "It is difficult, demanding work, but in the end it is enormously satisfying — and it can make a major impact on neonatal health."

>>> career at a glance

Ronald W. Davis, MD, MPH

1995–Present	**Director** Center for Health Promotion and Disease Prevention, Henry Ford Health System
1991–1995	**Chief Medical Officer** Michigan Department of Public Health
1987–1991	**Director** Office on Smoking and Health, National Center for Chronic Disease Prevention and Health Promotion, Centers for Disease Control and Prevention
1986–1987	**Medical Epidemiologist** Division of Health Education, National Center for Health Promotion and Education, Centers for Disease Control and Prevention
1984 –1986	**Epidemic Intelligence Service Officer** Division of Immunization, National Center for Prevention Services, Centers for Disease Control and Prevention

1 http://my.webmd.com/content/article/1728.54126
2 http://www.cossa.org/cahtbssrtestimony.html
3 http://www.cdc.gov/nccdphp/pe_factsheets/pe_tobacco_longdesc.htm
4 http://www.cdc.gov/tobacco/sgr/sgr_1986/SGR1986-Chapter6.pdf
5 http://www.cdc.gov/tobacco/sgr/sgr_1986/SGR1986-Chapter6.pdf
6 http://www.cdc.gov/idu/facts/Policy.htm
7 Personal communication, Dr. Ronald Davis, 12/17/01

THE MEDICINE/PUBLIC HEALTH INITIATIVE

Dr. Davis was elected to the American Medical Association's (AMA) Board of Trustees in June 2001. Because of his ties to both medicine and public health, he has been closely involved in an AMA-sponsored initiative that promotes the integration of medicine and public health. The Medicine/Public Health Initiative, which was launched in 1996 by the AMA and the American Public Health Association, was designed to bring together people who work in the fields of medicine and public health to explain and produce innovative solutions for the health problems of Americans. Its mission is to develop an agenda of action that engages public health and medicine in reshaping health education, research and practices.

The initiative's primary goals are:

○ Engaging the community

○ Changing the education process

○ Creating joint research efforts

○ Devising a shared view of health and illness

○ Working together in health care provision

○ Jointly developing health care assessment measures

○ Creating networks to translate initiative ideas into actions

Historically, many people have worked in both professions without bridging the two, Dr. Davis says. When he was working at the CDC and with the Michigan Department of Public Health, many of his colleagues had little, if any, association with the medical profession and vice versa. "Cooperation between these two disciplines is absolutely essential for the health of our patients," Dr. Davis says, "particularly in situations such as those that have arisen lately."

When responding to disasters or terrorism with biological or chemical agents, for example, Dr. Davis says, medicine and public health must work together to make sure that everyone involved is prepared to deal with these huge threats. In the case of anthrax or smallpox, the health care practitioner must be able to recognize a new case and report it quickly to the appropriate public health agencies. The public health agencies then need to confirm the diagnosis, which might involve sophisticated laboratory tests. Next, an epidemiologist will examine the pattern of reported cases in a particular locality to piece together whether the cases are isolated or widespread enough to be transmitted from place to place, which would occur with an infectious agent like smallpox. The public health agency will also be responsible for working with various partners in instituting treatments or guidelines for containment.

health educator

A TRUE TALE

Rima Rudd, MSPH, ScD, entered the field of public health in the 1960s, when she was actively engaged in organizing communities around political issues. She taught in New York City and also worked as an evaluator for

Rima Rudd, MSPH, ScD

the New York University (NYU) Department of Education. NYU had the contract to evaluate multiple projects that were funded through the War on Poverty efforts. In this important project, Dr. Rudd's interviewed participants and observed program activities that revolved around many of the barriers to adequate health care, food and housing faced by the poor. This experience sparked her interest in public health.

Dr. Rudd then worked in a free clinic in northern California, serving a population beleaguered by rising unemployment. At the same time, she was active in the women's

self-help movement. "That movement inspired much of my work," says Dr. Rudd. "I had a degree in English and philosophy and thought perhaps I ought to legitimize my work in community organizing — so I went back to school and obtained my master's in public health from the University of Massachusetts." While she was writing her thesis, she accepted a job as program designer for a model program funded by the Centers for Disease Control and Prevention, with the mission to design health programs in partnership with people in the local communities served.

Because of her interest in the broader policy implications of public health needs, Dr. Rudd was encouraged by the first Director of the Office of Health Promotion in the Surgeon General's office to pursue her doctorate. Dr. Rudd finished her doctoral studies at the Johns Hopkins School of Hygiene and Public Health, and interned in occupational health and safety, doing

> "An effective health educator requires both a set of varied skills and an ability to 'think outside the box.'"

most of her work in union settings. After working as an evaluator for a non-profit organization, Dr. Rudd accepted an academic appointment at the

Health Educator Checkpoint

Are you an "idea person" who is able to design, facilitate and implement educational programs?

Do your interests focus on pedagogy?

Do you have a talent for understanding the ethnic and cultural issues of different communities?

If so, read on

Massachusetts College of Pharmacy and then at Harvard. She is currently a member of the faculty in the Department of Health and Social Behavior at the Harvard School of Public Health, and also serves as Director of Educational Programs for the Health and Social Behavior Department.

Profiling the job

The work of public health educators (PHEs) is to change policies and environments as well as attitudes and behavior that affect health, and to operate in close association with community groups. PHEs plan and direct programs, design workshops and forums, work with community groups, and serve a broad public health agenda. They may conduct studies of public health education needs, evaluate the materials and methods used in programs, determine program effectiveness, and try to improve the general health in communities. They might do this by working with people and organizations addressing health-related issues such as pollution, drug abuse, nutrition, safety and stress management. These professionals also write health education materials such as fact sheets, pamphlets and brochures — a special and critical skill, as materials must often match the needs, preferences, and skills of underserved populations. According to Dr.

Rudd, public health education probably has its greatest impact in raising awareness, providing information, supporting and leading advocacy efforts, and sharing and augmenting skills. For example, health education is important in preventing chronic diseases such as diabetes and cardiovascular diseases. Learning more about diet, exercise, tobacco use and other lifestyle choices, and modifying behavior accordingly, can help to prevent, control and treat these diseases and reduce the risk of complications.

Public health educators work in a variety of settings with an array of agencies, businesses, and schools to develop and deliver educational programs. For example, a PHE might counsel factory workers about protecting themselves from pollution in the workplace, teach teenagers about how to prevent sexually transmitted diseases, or partner with families of patients who are recovering from heart attacks.

A public health educator benefits from a background in a variety of disciplines including biostatistics, epidemiology, environmental health sciences, health policy and the social and behavioral sciences. Needed skills include the ability to design assessments, conduct surveys, develop programs, plan budgets, train staff, oversee program activities, and conduct evaluations with both qualitative and quantitative methods. Furthermore, an understanding of pedagogy and social and behavioral theory is critical to crafting health-promoting programs. As an example of the broad interdisciplinary cooperation that goes into a public health effort, Dr. Rudd cites "Sisters Together." This national program began as an effort to design a model campaign to promote increased physical activity and healthful eating among women and was funded by the National Institute of Diabetes & Digestive & Kidney Diseases (NIDDK). Dr. Rudd and her colleagues first conducted a needs assessment by interviewing nutritionists at all community health centers in the city of Boston and by engaging in a thorough literature review of academic publications, popular magazines and programs. As it turned out, there were no programs addressing the problem of obesity prevention among African American women. As a result, the team engaged in in-depth formative research and conducted focus groups with community women, interviews with community leaders and staff members in local organizations, and toured the neighborhoods to identify existing resources. These activities helped structure the effort. Finally, the planning group began a community-wide effort to implement activities in full partnership with existing local organizations and local leaders. "Sisters Together" was cited as one of the ten model programs in the first Surgeon General's Report on Physical Activity. It has been replicated in several states and is now a national program.

Health literacy

Although Dr. Rudd is a health educator whose work centers on the design and evaluation of public heath programs for planned social change, a good deal of her current work focuses on health literacy. Dr. Rudd brings attention to the definition of functional literacy provided in the National Literacy Act of 1991: "The ability to read, write, and speak in English, and compute and solve problems at levels of proficiency necessary to function on the job and in society, to achieve one's goals, and develop one's knowledge and potential." She applies the definition of health literacy from Healthy People 2010: "The degree to which individuals have the capacity to obtain, process, and understand basic health information and services needed to make appropriate

Did you know?
It is estimated that low health literacy costs the health care system approximately $73 billion annually. The primary reasons are longer hospital stays or re-hospitalization and reduced access to health services.[1]

health decisions." She also notes that people's ability to use the spoken and written language to comprehend, act on and effectively use health information is a component of health literacy.

Although most of her work is public health, Dr. Rudd also focuses on health literacy in medical care settings. "Unfortunately, the greatest burden for obtaining access to health care is placed on the individual who may not have strong health literacy skills," Dr. Rudd says. "Access to services often depends on a literacy test under the guise of hard-to-manage forms or instructions." In addition, people with average functional literacy skills can easily make errors about medication or may not be able to comfortably

engage in discussions with professionals. This may be due to limited literacy skills, limited background information, and/or to an overuse of medical terms or professional jargon.

She notes that many public health and medical professionals do not speak in plain language. "While it is true that many patients may have difficulty understanding appointment slips, directions for medications or informed consent documents," says Dr. Rudd, "these materials are often poorly written. We have found that these materials often test out at grade levels that far exceed the reading ability of the average adult. I think a large part of the problem is that professionals are inadvertently gearing the documents to inappropriate reading levels."

According to Dr. Rudd, the only way to truly remedy the problem is to work on two levels at once. "We must improve our own communication skills as health professionals and we must support adult education, so people who have missed out on opportunities, for whatever reason, get another chance." She speaks highly of her grandmother, who came to this country at the age of 19, was fluent in three languages, but was unable to read any of them. "She was politically astute, a hard worker, a union organizer, and raised a very productive and healthy family. She was incredibly bright, but she never had schooling." Survival in today's society is not as in Dr. Rudd's grandmother's day, because modern American society requires literacy skills. Generally, to be fully functional in today's society, some experts believe that people need the reading skills of at least a ninth-grade education.[3] But half of the U.S. population has reading skills below that level. This fact must be part of public health planning. Fortunately, adult literacy programs in every state provide powerful venues for affecting change in the health of our populations.

A day in the life

As a public health educator, Dr. Rudd characterizes herself as an academic, a position she feels gives her the latitude to positively affect the health of the public. She works within public health, medical, and academic settings, often serving as principal investigator on studies that focus on the relationships among health, health information and adult education. She is as likely to be in the field as in the classroom.

"Research and program evaluations are core components of what I do," says Dr. Rudd. In developing the model program for "Sisters Together," for example, she attended community walking events, participated in needs assessments, and played an active role in evaluating the efficacy of the program design. "My job varies from project to project and often takes me out into the community, which is always a part of my work," she says.

On an average day, Dr. Rudd teaches a class [it might be "Innovative Strategies in Health Education," "Health Literacy" or "Planned Social Change"], confers with her staff and students on their health literacy work, sends e-mail messages to other scholars about shared research, meets with other faculty members, and participates in different university committees. She is a valued mentor to the next generation of health literacy scholars.

In explaining the role of a health educator who specializes in evaluation, Dr. Rudd cites a former student currently employed as an evaluator for hospital-funded community programs. "One of her programs is geared toward improving asthma patients' understanding of their condition and how to manage it," says Dr. Rudd. The program is also designed to address the broader environmental factors contributing to asthma in schools, households and the community, and to heighten awareness of asthma as a community health problem. "The educator also oversees a program aimed at improving

"Access to services often depends on a literacy test under the guise of hard-to-manage forms or instructions."

Rima Rudd, MSPH, ScD

the birth outcomes as well as maternal and infant health of high-risk families by providing information, referrals, advocacy and support services," says Dr. Rudd.

"Although the educator has an office in the hospital, much of her time is spent in the community," Dr. Rudd says. "She works with community agencies to help them design evaluation plans and tools to measure the effectiveness of their programs, and to use the information gathered to strengthen these programs."

>>> >> ## career at a glance

Rima Rudd, MSPH, ScD

1990–Present	**Lecturer on Health Education, Director of Educational Programs** for the Department of Health and Social Behavior, Harvard School of Public Health
2001–Present	**Co-Investigator** Literacy in Arthritis Management: A Randomized, Control Trial of a Novel Patient Education Intervention, RBB Arthritis and Musculoskeletal Diseases Clinical Research Center.
1996–Present	**Principal Investigator** Health and Adult Learning and Literacy research project, the National Center for the Study of Adult Learning and Literacy
1986–1990	**Evaluator** AIDS Professional Education Programs, JSI, Inc.
1987–1989	**Assistant Professor of Humanities** College of Pharmacy
1978–1980	**Program Designer** Lifeways Health Promotion Organization
1972–1975	**Director of Community Education Programs** Our Health Center
1970–1971, 1964–1969	**English Teacher** Walton High School, High School of Art and Design, Bronx, New York
1969–1970	**Evaluator** War on Poverty Programs, NYU Evaluation Team

1 http://www.gse.harvard.edu/~ncsall/research/learner.htm
2 http://www.agingsociety.org/healthlit.htm
3 http://www.nlm.nih.gov/pubs/cbm/hliteracy.html

mental health researcher

A TRUE TALE

Mindy Fullilove, MD, is a research psychiatrist at the New York State Psychiatric Institute and Professor of Clinical Psychiatry and Public Health at the Mailman School of Public Health at Columbia University. After graduating from Bryn Mawr College in 1971 with a degree in history, Dr. Fullilove obtained a master's degree in nutrition from Columbia University, and then received her medical degree from the Columbia University's College of Physicians and Surgeons in New York in 1978. She was a resident in psychiatry at New York Hospital's Westchester Division and Montefiore Hospital. She worked as a staff psychiatrist at the Morrisania Neighborhood Family Care Center in the Bronx, New York.

Mindy Fullilove, MD

Mental Health Researcher Checkpoint

Are you interested in the field of mental illness?

Are you willing to accept progress in small increments of success?

Are you interested in the physical and social diseases that can affect the quality of people's lives?

Do you believe you can change people's lives for the better through research?

If so, read on

In the mid-1980s, Dr. Fullilove left New York for San Francisco for a position on the faculty at the University of California at San Francisco (UCSF). Her interest in public health began when she worked in a San Francisco community mental health clinic. "The conditions of the clients were extremely poor. Mental health services were so underfunded that we couldn't do much of the work we knew needed to be done," she says. Dr. Fullilove determined that the only way she could improve things for the neighborhood, the clinic and the clients was through research, which she hoped would ultimately lead to the creation of new programs and new policies in mental health.

"Good mental health is related to how people live together. Not too surprisingly, a supportive, nurturing community or group seems to be the ideal environment for the development of healthy minds."

In 1986, Dr. Fullilove conceived of and founded the Medical Scholars Program at UCSF — a program that provided academic support to minority and female medical students. As co-principal investigator of the UCSF Center for AIDS Prevention Studies, she directed the minority component of the center, called Multicultural Inquiry and Research on AIDS (MIRA). She also served as principal investigator for several projects,

including "AIDS in Multiethnic Neighborhoods," an epidemiological investigation of HIV seroprevalence and risk behavior prevalence in 1,700 single
adult residents of San Francisco.

In 1990, Dr. Fullilove and her husband Robert were recruited by Columbia
University. In time he became Associate Dean for Community and Minority
Affairs at the Mailman School of Public Health, and she became a professor
at the School of Public Health and a research psychiatrist at the New York
State Psychiatric Institute.

Profiling the job

Within the field of public health, there are three distinct but overlapping
divisions of mental health: clinical practice, agency-based practice and
research. In clinical practice, professionals generally care for the individual
needs of indigent patients in settings that vary from hospitals to group homes
to clinics. Patients are cared for by a variety of mental health professionals
in these settings. Psychiatrists and psychologists do initial assessments, run
groups and implement behavioral intervention plans. Psychiatric nurses provide primary care nursing and often run education groups. Social workers
do psychosocial assessments, used to develop treatment plans, and also do
discharge planning.

Agency-based practice can have an educational component, such as the
training of teachers, parents and others to recognize the signs of mental distress
in children. Also, agencies provide programs that support specific populations, for example women who are dealing with the stresses of motherhood.
A good case to consider is that of a young mother who is poor, single and
feels overburdened by the demands of her new situation, Dr. Fullilove says.
A measure as simple as a nurse visiting the new mother's home can have a
dramatic impact and help minimize the risk of post-partum depression.

Research, the focus of Dr. Fullilove's work, is the third area. Much of the
mental health research she conducts is aimed at helping other public health
professionals understand the structure of communities as an essential pre-
cursor to the development and implementation of meaningful public health
outreach. Dr. Fullilove has done research on a wide array of topics related
to "place," particularly in poverty-stricken communities, where she has
studied physical and social diseases including AIDS, tuberculosis, asthma,
substance abuse and violence, in an effort to understand how these diseases
and conditions relate to the environment.

In the course of this work, Dr. Fullilove developed a theory she calls *the psychology of place*. Her theory sets forth the fundamental psychological connections people make to their environment — how people work, func-

tion and adapt within groups, how their need to create a common life within the group is met, and how they react when their environment is altered.

Dr. Fullilove's theory describes three fundamental processes common to people in all cultures. First, people have an emotional connection to where they live, a process she calls "place attachment." Second, in any human environment, people have to understand where they are, which in Dr. Fullilove's work is known as "orientation." Third, people's identities arise in part from the place they are in. For example, if you live in New York, part of your identity is as a New Yorker. People who move often experience stress because they must disconnect and reconnect on all three levels.

Additionally, people in a particular space belong to many different groups that interact in unique ways over time. For example, the simple community habit of buying a paper at the local newsstand each morning and saying "hello" to the other people buying their newspapers makes the newsstand a crossroads of the neighborhood, Dr. Fullilove says. This applies as well to schools, churches, banks, grocery stores, dry cleaners, apartment buildings, houses, streets and parks.

Dr. Fullilove's research came to the fore on September 11, 2001, when the World Trade Center collapsed, taking with it the lives of more than 2,800 people. According to Dr. Fullilove, the obliteration of a neighborhood that was home and workplace to so many may mirror in its consequences the losses experienced during urban renewal in the '50s and '60s, when entire city neighborhoods were bulldozed. People were uprooted and lost the connection to their "place." Even 50 years later, she says, urban renewal projects still have negative repercussions. "My fear on September 11 was, and indeed still is, that the loss of place and home will continue to affect the mental health of the affected for decades to come."

With so many work places destroyed, companies were dispersed. "They are now scattered all over, and this leads to an absolute loss of social connections." In order to repair social connections and prevent mental illness, Dr. Fullilove and her multidisciplinary research team of psychologists, psychiatrists, social workers, mental health nurses, health educators, sociologists and other public health practitioners has established "NYC Recovers," an alliance of organizations working for the social and emotional recovery of New York City.

A day in the life

Popular notions notwithstanding, not all mental health professionals treat patients, interpret dreams or divide their days into 50-minute sessions. Dr. Fullilove is a terrific example.

Much of Dr. Fullilove's week is taken up with research projects that affect the daily lives of thousands of people in New York City. She is currently principal investigator on a project entitled, "Root Shock: The Long-term Consequences of African American Dispossession." The project aims at assessing the continuing impact of urban renewal conducted in the 1950s and 60s. She has also served as principal investigator in "Case Study of School Violence," a research project funded by the National Research Council in 2001 to examine lethal school violence in East New York, and in "Coming Home: an Evaluation of the Bradhurst Project," funded by the Centers for Disease Control and Prevention, and designed as a longitudinal study of housing resettlement in central Harlem.

When she's not immersed in research, Dr. Fullilove is likely to be teaching, writing or discussing future projects with public health consultants or community groups. Lately she's been devoting significant time to her work on the 15-member National Task Force for Community Preventive Services, which is collaborating with the CDC on an evidence-based guidebook to public health practice. Each task force member is responsible for contributing one or more chapters in a specific area of public health practice. Dr. Fullilove's chapters address violence prevention and the sociocultural environment.

"We have high hopes that our work will add to the public health profession's understanding of the psychological impacts of displacement and violence," says Dr. Fullilove of her research. "Ideally, policy and funding to deal with these traumas will follow, to heal and nurture the mental health of whole communities."

career at a glance

Mindy Fullilove, MD

2000–Present	**Professor of Clinical Psychiatry and Public Health** Columbia University
1990–Present	**Research Psychiatrist** New York State Psychiatric Institute
1986–1990	**Director** Multicultural Inquiry and Research on AIDS, Bayview-Hunter's Point Foundation, San Francisco, CA
1986–1990	**Director** Medical Scholars Program, UCSF School of Medicine
1983–1986	**Staff Psychiatrist** Bayview-Hunter's Point Foundation
1982–1983	**Director** Day Treatment, Morrisania Neighborhood Family Care Center, Bronx, N.Y.

1 http://www.nami.org/fact/htm

health communications
communications specialist

**Communica-
tions Specialist
Checkpoint**

Are you
a creative and
resourceful
person?

Are you
comfortable
working in
all aspects of
the media?

Would you
enjoy going
into local
communities
to disseminate
information
about health
programs you
have designed?

If so, read on

A TRUE TALE

It was strictly by chance that Thomas Valente, PhD, came to work in the field of public health. He began his student career as a math major at Mary Washington College in Fredericksburg, Virginia. "My program was in theoretical mathematics so I never took a statistics class, which, when you consider it, is quite unusual for someone in this field." He now believes it was actually fortuitous he chose math. "To work well in health communications," he says, "you need to understand prevalences and incidences of diseases as well as determinants of outcomes. Formal training in math theory is good preparation for such work."

Thomas W. Valente, PhD

Dr. Valente received his master's degree in mass communications from San Diego State University and went on to the Annenberg School for Communication at the University of Southern California (USC), where he received his PhD in Communication. He believes his thesis, *Mathematical Models of the Diffusion of Innovation,* a well-known theory in public health, earned him his first job as an evaluation officer at the Johns Hopkins Bloomberg School of Public Health.

Dr. Valente's wife, who is a native Californian, eventually wanted to move back to the West Coast. At that time, USC was looking for someone to direct its new Master of Public Health program. Dr. Valente got the job. Today, he is the Director of the MPH program in the USC School of Medicine and an associate professor in the school's Department of Preventive Medicine.

"Given the option to change or not, most people will opt for the status quo. Typically, motivators and stimuli are needed to successfully alter habits."

Profiling the job

Effective public health communication encourages people to change certain attitudes, beliefs or behaviors so that they adopt better health practices and ultimately improve their health. Such lifestyle changes, however, do not always come easily. "Given the option to change or not, most people will opt for the status quo," says Dr. Valente. "Typically, motivators and stimuli are needed to successfully alter habits."

Four of the most useful channels for public health communication are interpersonal communications, print publications, electronic communications and mass media. Interpersonal communications programs consist of the training of counselors and providers as well as the recruitment of lay health advisors to conduct associated outreach activities. Print publications consist of flyers, brochures, billboards, newspaper advertisements and many other types of printed matter. Electronic communications are increasingly being used to send messages to targeted and general lists of people, and the Internet now contains numerous web sites devoted to health information. The mass media consist of advertising campaigns, films, music and television, where health messages embedded in entertainment educate consumers.

Entertainment-education, often referred to as "Enter-Educate," is a health communication strategy that uses entertainment media to inform audiences about health issues. Through street plays — or street theater — where "the world is the stage," the message is carried to the target population by way of vignettes performed in public arenas. For example, an Enter-Educate program initiated in Peru featured a 20-minute play, acted by local citizens, to promote modern contraceptive methods to young couples. In the play, "Ms. Rumors" feeds incorrect information to a young couple that wants to wait to have children, but is interrupted constantly by a pharmacist and others who present the correct information in an entertaining way. The troupes travel through cities and towns in a parade, gathering their audience as they go. Eventually they stop, raise a small backdrop and put on the performance. At each performance, counselors are available to answer questions before and after the play. Approximately 200,000 people saw street theater performances in Lima and in other cities and provinces of Peru during the Enter-Educate program.[2] This reproductive health communication campaign was run by APROPO (Support to Population Programs), a Peruvian non-governmental organization, and supported by USAID, with technical assistance provided by the Johns Hopkins Center for Communication Programs. "Health communications programs need to be developed appropriately for both the successful delivery of their messages and culturally for the audience they serve," says Dr. Valente. "The Peruvian street play program was a splendid example of a health communication tailored ethnically for its

Did you know?
Soap operas taught an estimated 48% of their 38 million regular viewers something about diseases and how to prevent them, a 1999 CDC Healthstyles Survey revealed. Over one-third of viewers took some action as a result.[1]

audience and designed as well to reach a market which does not necessarily have access to electronic media sources."

Other entertainment media, such as theater, film, radio and television soap operas have been a common form of entertainment-education in developing and developed countries for the promotion of family planning, reproductive health and female empowerment. Recently, the popular television series *ER* inserted spots about contraceptive use into their program. One *ER* episode addressed contraception through a storyline about a character who asked physicians and nurses in the emergency room what to do to prevent pregnancy. The vignette lasted only three minutes, and the information dispensed about

birth control pills took only 20 seconds of that time. But a follow-up viewer survey, underwritten by the Henry J. Kaiser Family Foundation in Menlo Park, California, showed a 17 percent rise in *ER*-viewers' awareness of a woman's options for preventing pregnancy.[3] Globally, similar campaigns are underway. A production company in Uganda recently ran a 13-part television drama focused on helping young adults make health decisions about family planning. In Ethiopia, a radio serial drama used characters and a storyline to encourage young adults to protect themselves from HIV/AIDS.

"To deliver effective results, practitioners must constantly measure what works and what does not work. Pre- and post-program samplings are useful evaluation tools."

Another integral yet distinct concept in public health communications is "social marketing" — the planning and implementing of programs designed to bring about social change. While the consensus is that social marketing emphasizes non-tangible ideas and practices, Dr. Valente views social marketing as still more effective when product-based. "But," he says, "the types of products I refer to are those which improve health-related behavior, like condoms."

Communication is not only about creating programs. Successful practice in the field also mandates that you evaluate the programs you have created. "To deliver effective results, practitioners must constantly measure what works and what does not work," says Dr. Valente. "Pre- and post-program surveys of the target audience are the minimum evaluation needs." For example, if the California Department of Health wanted to evaluate an anti-tobacco campaign, it would select a random sample of the state population, and then interview the sample about their smoking behaviors, attitudes and perceptions about smoking. After the campaign was broadcast, the sample would be interviewed again to determine if their attitudes or behaviors had changed and if those changes were prompted by the campaign. Mass media programs can also be evaluated through the more rigorous methodology of longitudinal studies set up to track people's knowledge, attitudes and practices over specified periods of time.

A day in the life

As director and administrator of the MPH program within the University of Southern California Keck School of Medicine, Dr. Valente divides his time among three main activities: administrative duties, public health research and teaching. Communication is central to all three of those areas — and to the very notion of public health, he says. But what does a day in the life of a public health communications specialist look like? Dr. Valente describes the daily schedule of a communications specialist supervising a pregnancy prevention project managed by a state health department.

When he arrives at his office in the morning, the latest statewide epidemiological studies of teenage pregnancy are on his desk. To get this information out to the media in the most efficient way, the specialist holds a staff meeting to discuss and brainstorm the talking points the department wants to see in print, on television and on the Internet. The team also discusses how best to get their message out directly to the public, and through the health centers themselves. In both cases, Dr. Valente notes, complicated research data and results must be transformed into engaging and relevant lay language.

In the afternoon, the communications specialist meets with health workers from different districts, as well as community workers, leaders and volunteers, who may include Girl Scout troop leaders, school nurses and members of the county board of health. He also works on creating a program that

Did you know?
Social marketing was formalized in the 1970s when Philip Kotler and Gerald Zaltman realized the same marketing principles used to sell commercial products could be used to influence human behavior. [4]

addresses teen pregnancy through traditional methods such as access to health care and sexuality education. As part of this undertaking, the communications specialist creates a cadre of people in the field able to return to their health centers and make the same presentation to their peers.

That evening the communications officer addresses the local school board meeting on the subject of an adolescent sexuality program, offering assistance and guidance in implementing a program. The officer and aides distribute brochures to the school board and public that reinforce the messages. "Public health is about using every possible avenue for educating the public," says Dr. Valente. "Without communications — and communications professionals — public health as we know it couldn't exist."

career at a glance

Thomas W. Valente, PhD

2000–Present	**Associate Professor** Department of Preventive Medicine, School of Medicine, University of Southern California, Los Angeles, California
2000–Present	**Member** Institute of Medicine Panel, "Assuring the Health of the Public in the 21st Century"
1991–2000	**Assistant to Associate Professor** Department of Population & Family Health Sciences, Bloomberg School of Public Health, Johns Hopkins University, Baltimore, MD **Director,** Health Communication Program

1 http://www.cdc.gov/communication/healthsoap.htm
2 http://www.jhuccp.org/centerpubs/sp_9/pg26.stm
3 www.kff.org/content/archive/1358/ers.html
4 http://www.social-marketing.com/whatis.html

health communications
journalist

A TRUE TALE

George Strait, an award-winning health and science reporter, has an under-graduate degree in biology from Boston University and studied biochemical

George Strait

genetics at Atlanta University. He says that academic work provided him with a firm footing in the scientific process and method, and a good understanding of how to interpret clinical studies. It also gave him enough command of scientific terminology so that later, when he had the opportunity to approach scientists as a journalist, he was able to speak their language. The one thing his studies did *not* provide him right out of school was a job.

As a result, after graduation in 1969 Strait found employment driving a cab in Atlanta. Little did he know at the time that one of his "fares" would be a trip to his future. "As luck would have it, the person in my cab was going to the building where my wife worked. I stopped in to say hello to her and happened to meet someone who told me the radio station upstairs, the number one rock and roll radio station in Atlanta, was looking for a disk jockey." Strait was introduced to the general manager who took him into the production studio for an audition. The next night he was on the air playing rock and roll records from midnight-to-six. Soon he met the news director of the corresponding television station, who put him on TV to broadcast sports. By the time Strait left Atlanta several years later, he was anchoring the evening news. Things continued to move quickly, and eventually Strait came to Washington, DC, to join ABC-TV. Searching for a way to attract viewers, the producers created a news segment called *The American Agenda* (the program is now called *A Closer Look*) and, in part because of his science background, assigned Strait several segments on health issues. The segments were so well received that ABC offered him a permanent position. In 1984, he was named the Chief Medical Reporter for *World News Tonight.* At that time, there had never been a specialized medical reporter on any network, making George Strait the first. For the next 16 years, his varied and distinguished reports and special programs on health appeared regularly on ABC's *World News Tonight* and *Nightline.* During that time,

Journalist Checkpoint

Can you produce under very tight deadlines?

Can you write well and fast?

Do you think you would enjoy "chasing a story," which involves basic research as well as tracking down and interviewing the experts?

If so, read on

he twice received the industry's highest award, the Alfred I. duPont Award, for a groundbreaking series on women's health and a documentary on AIDS in minority communities.

Although he does not have a public health degree, George Strait is considered an important figure in health and is often referred to as "public health's ambassador-at-large." In his prior position as health reporter, he covered many health stories that he remembers well. "Some reports have been more memorable than others," says Strait. As far as sheer numbers he says he has covered more stories about the HIV/AIDS epidemic than any other. "This global epidemic has forced all of us to rethink our prejudices, how we deliver public health, and our roles as citizens of the world. It has been both the most gratifying and difficult story for me to cover."

> "There are three basic requirements to being a good health reporter: You must be curious, be able to write a coherent sentence and be able to tell a good story. If you have those, you are 90 percent of the way there."

In his current job as a consultant to the Kaiser Family Foundation, he continues to assess health-related and scientific information and disseminate it in an effort to prevent disease, promote health awareness and achieve overall good public health.

Profiling the job

Being a television health and medical correspondent is not that different from any other news job, Strait says, but it carries different responsibilities. As the expert for the media outlet, you essentially act as an information interpreter and filter. Because of his expertise and years of training, Strait was able to tell if a health study was important or not, if the information being released was new or recycled, and how significant a breakthrough it might be. "Health reporting is really a question of finding information and assessing it," he says, "It requires trying to ferret out the truth and trying to fairly present what you learn."

In general, reported health information is gathered from a number of different sources, including physicians, scientists, health departments, government health agencies and medical journals. As a correspondent, Strait spent much of his time contacting health experts to discuss the impact of major clinical trials and other findings. Although the primary source of health information for the public is the health care community, a recent study suggested that nearly 50 percent of the American public gets their health information from the news media.[1] "The critical part of that study is that, at some point in time, 30 percent of those people who got their information from the news media actually acted on it." That surprised Strait. "Most people don't decide whom to vote for based on what one Congressional correspondent or

one White House correspondent reports, but people actually make, in some cases, life-and-death decisions based on what one health reporter has to say."

As a result, a health reporter must be concerned with how people hear what is said. For example, if you or a loved one has breast cancer and there is a breast cancer story on the news, it is going to grab your attention. The health reporter needs to present an accurate and balanced report and make sure it is not distorted or sensationalized. "You never know who is in your audience or how what you say will affect them. If you report on a breakthrough to treat multiple sclerosis, you have to know that someone with multiple sclerosis is going to want to hear that the treatment works."

Strait says there are three basic requirements to being a good health reporter: curiosity, the ability to write a coherent sentence and the ability to tell a good story. If you have those, he says, you are 90 percent of the way to being an effective journalist. That there is no special training or credentialing required to be a health reporter is unfortunate, Strait believes. "Some of the most egregious errors in health reporting are made by people who have no sense of the context in which material should be delivered. Most of the weather forecasters on local television and radio channels have met the requirements of the Seal of Approval program of the American Meteorological Association. I don't think you need to have been an elected official to cover politics, and I don't think that you need to have been in the military to cover the Pentagon. But reporting science and health is different. I think a reporter should be required to understand the context in which the data is given."

Strait suggests that public health students and professionals wishing to enter the field of radio and television broadcasting or newspaper reporting can do so via two major routes. Academically, he says, they should consider a master's degree in communications or journalism, which would provide them with an excellent background and hold them in good stead with any media organization. The other route, he says, is the guild method – that is, on-the-job training. "An aspiring health reporter might want to apply for an internship somewhere. I would suggest he or she contact a local communications outfit, be it newspaper, television or radio and arrange an interview with an editor or news director."

Most recently Mr. Strait was Senior Vice President of Media Distribution for The Dr. Spock Company, an integrated Internet media company that provides parents with the latest expert advice, information and inspiration on raising happy, healthy children. The company combines the philosophy of the pediatrician Dr. Benjamin Spock with up-to-date parenting information from leading authorities in parenting and children's health. "Two years ago — a lifetime in the Internet world — there were more than 1,700 health-related websites, yet there was little chance that anyone reading them could tell whether or not the information was any good." With an increasing number of people going to the Web for their health information, Strait felt it was extremely important to provide accurate health information. In order to do that, he would need a good platform. "Dr. Spock is trusted," Strait says. "Three generations of people have been raised with his books." Strait was hired to evaluate the content on the Dr. Spock website. "I saw it as an opportunity to ensure that all the content was transparent, that people knew where it came from and could trust what it said. If we were successful, we would then be able to show the rest of the Internet world how to do it correctly."

Reporting on the Internet is no different from television reporting, Strait says. The Web has an advantage, however, because there are no space constraints. You can write an article, but you can also link that article to much of the information that exists in the world on that specific topic. Strait says a reporter's major concern is time and space — whether there is sufficient time to get the facts and sufficient space to report them. Will 30 seconds, a minute-and-a-half, two column inches or even a full page be adequate? On the Web, you may still have a deadline, but you never have a space problem.

Currently, Mr. Strait is a private consultant for the Kaiser Family Foundation, an independent national health philanthropy dedicated to providing information and analysis on health issues to policy makers, the media and the general public.

A day in the life

Until recently, George Strait was a health and science reporter for ABC-TV in New York. While the structure of his days was fairly uniform, he says, what he saw and wrote about was anything but.

"I'd typically begin my workday at home, around 7:30am, with the delivery of *The Washington Post, The New York Times* and *The Wall Street Journal,*" he says. "I'd read them, searching for story ideas, then get to the ABC studios around nine and read another paper." Next he turned his attention to the medical journals. "Each day of the week a different medical journal comes out — *The New England Journal of Medicine* on Thursdays, *JAMA* on Wednesdays, and so on. I'd peruse them carefully in search of 'the next new thing.'"

Based on what he had learned, Strait would pitch a story idea to his editor. "It could be about almost anything related to medicine and health — allergies, a new treatment for HIV, newly discovered health risks." At 10:00am, senior network executives and editorial staff around the world dialed into a company-wide conference call to discuss the story lineup for that evening's *World News Tonight*. "As soon as my story got the green light, I went off to track it down," says Strait.

Strait and the video crew would locate their sources, conduct interviews and videotape the story. Then Strait would sit down to write the script. When it was finished, he sent it to editors in Washington and New York for approval. Finally, he recorded the narration as the producer and the videotape operator assembled all of the pieces. By 6:30pm, he was on the air with the full segment.

"I think the basic responsibility of a reporter is to tell as much as he or she knows about any given subject, in the time in which they have to study it. Some people get years to work on one story. Some people get minutes. You have to be able to go with what you have."

George Strait

"I got used to digging out the facts, scripting and reporting stories under extremely tight deadlines," he recalls. "But some deadlines were tighter than others." Late one August afternoon, he remembers, "my boss called to say we'd be covering a story about biological weapons and that our Pentagon guy was going to handle it, but that he wanted me to do a story about what the weapons actually do to the human body. It was 4:30pm; airtime was 6:30pm. Meanwhile, this was August, when nobody is around."

After panicking briefly, Strait jumped in with both feet. "Somehow, I was lucky enough to find an expert who just happened to be in town, got him to the studio and interviewed him. We found some pictures and had the graphics people make up some visuals to go with the story. Somehow, we got it done and the story worked. It was two hours of pure terror, but at the same time, great fun, and incredibly satisfying when it was over."

>>> career at a glance

George Strait

2001–Present	**Health and Media Consultant** Private Practice, Belmont, CA
2000–Present	**Member** Institute of Medicine Panel "Assuring the Health of the Public in the 21st Century"
2000–2001	**Senior Vice-President of Content and Media** The Dr. Spock Company, Menlo Park, CA
1999–2000	**Senior Counsel** IssueSphere, Nelson A.S., Inc., Washington, D.C.
1984–1999	**Chief Medical Correspondent** ABC News
1982–1984	**Special Projects Correspondent** ABC News
1978–1982	**White House Correspondent** ABC News
1977–1978	**General Assignment Correspondent** ABC News
1972–1976	**News Correspondent, Anchor** WPVI Philadelphia, PA
1969–1972	**Radio Disc Jockey, Television News, Sports and Weather Anchor** WQXI Atlanta, GA

1 Malone, M.E., The Boston Globe, "TV Remains Dominant Source for Americans on Medical Information"; March 12, 2002

practicing public health in a managed care setting

Did you ever stop to consider what is meant by the term "public" in public health? Any modern definition of public health must include a greater appreciation for the importance that populations play in determining the health of the public. Population groups are variable and include characteristics such as geography, race and ethnicity, income, age, disease and clinical conditions, and insurance status.

Reed V. Tuckson, MD

By Reed Tuckson, MD, Senior Vice-President of Consumer Health and Medical Care Advancement, UnitedHealth Group

UnitedHealth Group, a Minnesota-based national health and well being company, facilitates the provision of a variety of health care services to more than 35 million people. We believe that an important element in the delivery of quality health care includes understanding the dynamic relationship between individual health status and the population groups from which the individual arises. It has become very clear that the etiology of much of the disease burden in our nation results from, and is exacerbated by, the health-related behaviors of people and the environment in which they live. It is also clear that the prevention of disease, cost effective and precise diagnostic decision making, and effective comprehensive therapeutic interventions, are all significantly enhanced by sophistication in connecting the health of the individual to relevant realities of their population groups. This means asking compelling questions and looking for comprehensive answers. These questions involve issues such as: how local social pressures affect an individual's inclinations toward healthy living; the special genetic concerns that result from shared biology; the effect of age on medical and non-medical health-related decisions; and the community-wide environmental conditions that may comprise the root of a syndrome. The challenge and opportunity before all participants in health and medical care delivery is to maximize the interplay between individual health and public/population health to improve the efficiency and effectiveness of health interventions.

One of the challenges faced by today's public health practitioner is to gather data about a given population that supports actionable and effective intervention. This challenge is somewhat reduced when a practitioner works with a robust database of defined populations of subscribers or enrollees.

When we evaluate information in a database, we learn about the health characteristics and behaviors of groups of people as well as that of individuals. Aggregated information can be used proactively to identify individuals who are at special risk for poor outcomes and to target them for appropriate intervention. This process of gathering and analyzing population-based data to identify at risk and medically needy individuals is often referred to as "predictive modeling." By using mathematical algorithms, statisticians can now process large amounts of data to make predictions, decisions, and develop models and guidelines for interventions to apply to groups and individuals. This shift to a more population-based focus results not only in better health for individuals but in better health for communities. In addition, this shift leads to greater efficiency and cost effectiveness in health care delivery.

None of this is possible, of course, without a significant investment in computer systems and data software. In addition, effective intervention requires a team of professionals who are trained to make sense of the data and then interact with the people who have been identified as "in need." Public health informatics — information technology applied to the field of health care — is a critical element of our data assessment and is becoming more important each day.

A practical example of how this works comes from patients who have been diagnosed with both breast cancer and depression. Data analysis of a large number of such patients indicates a significant likelihood that they will not comply with their therapeutic regimen. Often, different members of a health care delivery team focus on only one diagnosis and may be unaware that the patient suffers from more than one disorder. The ability to use population-based data and analysis to predict that patients with breast cancer and depression are a population at risk avoids the fragmented approach that often exists in health care today and provides an opportunity to achieve better health care outcomes.

Population-based medicine is a bridge that connects the traditional public health system with today's comprehensive health and medical care management systems. Understanding behaviorioral and other social/environmental determinants of health provides opportunities to promote health, prevent disease and diagnose diseases more effectively. Sophisticated analysis of population-based data leads to anticipating therapeutic problems and influences medical care management.

Finally, population-based health care data facilitates coordination of care, fills gaps in health services delivery, and helps connect patients to necessary community-based resources. As a physician and a health care executive, I have believed, for years, that the partnership between the medical care system and the public health system is a natural one. If we embrace such a partnership, we can demonstrably enhance quality of life, improve the efficiency of health care delivery, and save lives every day.

Reed V. Tuckson, MD, is currently senior vice-president of Consumer Health and Medical Care Advancement, UnitedHealth Group, where he works with business groups to create new health care systems, enhance patient-physician relationships, improve medical care quality and assist individuals in optimizing their health. Prior to joining UnitedHealth Group, Dr. Tuckson served as senior vice-president, Professional Standards, for the American Medical Association. The former president of the Charles R. Drew University of Medicine and Science in Los Angeles from 1991 to 1997, Dr. Tuckson also served as senior vice-president for programs of the March of Dimes Birth Defects Foundation from 1990 to 1991. He was the commissioner of public health for the District of Columbia from 1986 to 1990.

Dr. Tuckson currently is a member of several health care-related and academic organizations, including the Institute of Medicine of the National Academy of Sciences. In addition, he currently serves as a member of the Secretary of Health's Advisory Committee on Genetic Testing and has held a number of other federal appointments, including seats on cabinet-level advisory committees on health reform, infant mortality, children's health, violence and radiation testing.

A graduate of Howard University and the Georgetown University School of Medicine, Dr. Tuckson trained as an intern, resident and fellow in General Internal Medicine at the Hospital of the University of Pennsylvania. A Robert Wood Johnson Clinical Scholar of the University of Pennsylvania, he also studied Health Care Administration and Policy at the Wharton School of Business and was active in ambulatory, student health, prevention and geriatric clinical care settings.

**Corporate
Medical
Director
Checkpoint**

Do you like
the idea of
working in
a corporate
setting?

Are you
interested in
working
conditions that
affect health?

Do you
understand the
connection
between prac-
ticing public
health and
keeping up
with the
changing cir-
cumstances of
doing business
in a foreign
country?

If so, read on

A TRUE TALE

Wayne Lednar, MD, PhD, graduated from Fordham University in New York with a degree in biology. After four years, he says, he knew what he did *not* want to do, and that was to "count hairs on mosquito legs." Rather, he

Wayne Lednar, MD, PhD

sought a way to combine his interest in biology with people and health. He learned from a classmate about the field of public health, an area that would enable him to use his science background to improve the health of specific populations. He then earned a master's degree in public health from the University of Massachusetts, where he specialized in environmental health.

Wanting to understand more about the field, Dr. Lednar attended the University of North Carolina, Chapel Hill, where he earned a PhD in epidemiology. "By that time," he says, "I could put the story together and

know what to recommend if things were not working. If I wanted to be able to ask good questions, understand each answer, and place each answer on the continuum of cause and effect, I felt I needed to know more about disease." That search for answers led him back to school, this time to The George Washington University in Washington, D.C., where he received a medical degree.

After an internship in pediatrics and a residency in general preventive medicine, Dr. Lednar spent the next ten years in the United States Army Medical Corps running residency programs to train physicians in the specialty of preventive medicine and public health at Walter Reed in Washington, D.C., and then at the Madigan Army Medical Center in Tacoma, Washington. In Tacoma, he was responsible for the public health support to a population of 40,000 soldiers and civilian employees, 100,000 family members of soldiers

"A large part of my job is to anticipate the demands of Kodak's operation and the capabilities of our employees. If we have a mismatch, people are going to get sick or they are going to get hurt."

and 160,000 military retirees. In 1988, after spending ten years in the service, the Eastman Kodak Company recruited Dr. Lednar to work in Rochester, New York, as Kodak's corporate epidemiologist. In 1995, he was promoted to Corporate Medical Director (CMD) for Kodak's worldwide operations, and in 2002 appointed a vice president.

Profiling the job

As Corporate Medical Director at Kodak, Dr. Lednar monitors the health of the company's workforce in every country in which Kodak operates, ensuring that Kodak's employees can perform their jobs effectively and safely. Much of this activity is predicated on understanding the individual needs of workers, what Kodak expects of them, and the kinds and quality of medical care resources available throughout the world. "We aim for a good match between the demands of work and the capabilities of our employees. If we have a mismatch," Dr. Lednar says, "people are going to get sick and they are going to get hurt. Our job is to anticipate this, and to design solutions within our initial job placement process and the way we operate our businesses, so that we have a wide safety margin between job demand and worker capability."

One way to avoid injury is by proper design of the workspace and the work system. Assembly line work systems that are poorly designed can lead to overwhelmed, stressed or injured employees and to defective products. "I remember the *I Love Lucy* episode from years ago where Lucy was working on an assembly line boxing pies, and the line went so fast she couldn't keep up — pies ended up flying all over the place. That's a comical but good example of how work systems can be set to produce a lot of product, but can simultaneously overwhelm the people who have to do the work. In the end, you have a substandard product, poor employee morale and a chance for accidents to happen." The field of occupational public health plays a key role in understanding the potential for illness and injury in business operations, and works with the people who can prevent poor outcomes from occurring. Those people include industrial engineers, time and motion study specialists, and even those who engineer the machinery and select the materials.

A still more effective approach to alleviating such on-the-job health risks would be to predict their occurrence *before* they occur, which is the subspecialty of trend analysis. Occupational safety and health work includes recognition of trends and response to them. A good example of such a trend is the countrywide increase in the number of adults who, for the first time in

Did you know?
The Occupational Safety and Health Administration's (OSHA) mission is to prevent work-related injuries, illnesses and deaths. Since the agency was created in 1971, OSHA estimates that occupational deaths have been cut in half and injuries have declined by 40 percent.[1]

their lives, have developed asthma.[2] "We need to be aware that this is occurring and to understand its root causes. If there are work-related contributions to those causes, then it's our job to modify or reduce them. If someone has asthma that's not caused by the work environment, we need to be certain that we do not make the condition worse," says Dr. Lednar. If part of an asthmatic employee's job involves working among mists, vapors, aerosols or other irritating particles in the workspace air, either the company needs to purify the air, supply adequate respiratory protection, such as respirators, or relocate the employee. We would not know that asthma is an evolving public health issue without trend monitoring, a population-based quantitative discipline of epidemiology, according to Dr. Lednar.

Kodak has manufacturing facilities in more than 20 countries around the world and does business in more than 140 countries. As CMD and manager of the worldwide network of medical departments at each of Kodak's factories, Dr. Lednar needs to know about the current health and safety issues specific to each country. Perhaps an infectious disease is linked to drinking water and local food supply. Perhaps there are personal safety issues. Because having a physician in smaller factories is not always feasible, Dr. Lednar sometimes staffs the local medical department with occupational health nurses. In addition to Kodak's commitment to the health care needs of its own employees, Kodak is strongly committed to operating in a way that does not adversely affect the environment or health of the population in its host communities. The management of the environmental impact of business operations is an essential component of occupational health.

Occupational and safety issues in office settings, while different from those of factories, are of no less concern to the occupational health specialist. The major health issues for office staff in businesses are musculoskeletal (back, wrist, upper extremity), mental (depression, anxiety, panic attack) and, as is true for any workforce containing a higher percentage of older workers, cardiovascular disease. Another common problem in working groups is respiratory disease, which Dr. Lednar calls a "three-part story," whose chapters are smoking-associated diseases such as Chronic Obstructive Pulmonary Disease and emphysema, asthma and infectious respiratory illnesses. The last is largely preventable. Infectious diseases such as influenza can abruptly affect a large proportion of a department in 24 hours. Using immunizations to anticipate and then to prevent a flu epidemic in the workplace is occupational medicine at its very best. As a result of such foresight, the workers stay healthy and business remains in operation, with at worst minimal loss to productivity.

Such excellent practice requires training that only certain degree programs provide. Students interested in occupational medicine would do well to have a Master's in Public Health (MPH). The required core courses can only enhance capabilities necessary to the field. "Perhaps surprisingly to some, the *behavioral* studies core is essential because in today's world, with the stresses placed on today's workers and their families, the health needs of our employees and family members are increasingly in the mental health area." Occupational safety and health integrates a number of disciplines: occupational medicine, occupational health nursing, industrial hygiene, toxicology, epidemiology, ergonomics and others. These combined disciplines mesh to serve any number of industries such as manufacturing, financial services and technology.

Occupational health professionals in the field can work in both the public and private sectors. One of the largest employers is the government, at the local, state and federal levels. Primary local concerns include the environmental health areas of sanitation, food safety and water safety. Most states have Occupational Safety and Health (OSH) departments or agencies, which conduct surveillance and inspections of workplaces, and have state registries where employers must (and employees and physicians should) report certain occupational diseases and injuries. The information is put into an epidemiological database that is monitored statewide. Another state government concern is the housing industry, where workers renovating older homes are sometimes at risk of lead contact from lead-based paint and workers on newer construction sites are at risk of general work-related accidents. States active in highway bridge repair must anticipate potential lead exposure in sandblasting painted bridge surfaces. At the federal level, employment opportunities exist in the National Institute for Occupational Safety and Health (NIOSH) and the Department of Labor. The Centers for Disease

"Using immunizations to anticipate and then to prevent a flu epidemic in the workplace is occupational medicine at its very best. As a result of such foresight, the workers stay healthy and business remains in operation, with at worst minimal loss to productivity."

Wayne Lednar, MD, PhD

Control and Prevention (CDC) has OSH-related opportunities. The mission of OSHA, the federal Occupational Safety and Health Administration, is to protect American workers.

In the private sector, professionals can find employment in the transportation business, where concerns center on baggage handlers, subway and bus drivers, and air traffic controllers, the last notably subject to severe stress. Even financial services require the services of an OSH professional. "Occupational health is not just concerned with people falling off a scaffold or getting burned," Dr. Lednar says. "Actually the workplace is getting physically safer. But the pressure on people to perform and complete a day's work has sent the stress level soaring. This, too, is one of our concerns." Another OSH concern is business travelers who fly frequently and the special stresses they face crossing time zones continually and encountering the heightened security precautions due to terrorism.

A day in the life

As corporate medical director for Kodak, Dr. Lednar faces a complex array of daily challenges. He meets with representatives from health insurance companies, with whom he discusses company health plans and the health needs of Kodak families. He might then have a teleconference with his medical director in Brazil to evaluate and discuss programs and any problems, any measures that have been taken since the last such conference, priorities for future programs and how company management might respond. Next on his itinerary is preparing a group of executives traveling to a different part of the world on company business. He instructs them on how to stay safe in their foreign destination, makes sure they have had the proper immunizations and advises them on how to contact a local physician who will provide care if necessary. He also provides background information on the country to which the executives are traveling. After preparing the traveling group, there might be a discussion with federal relations staff members from the Washington, D.C. office about pending health care legislation and how it might impact Kodak.

A medical director working in a factory setting has responsibilities distinctly different from Dr. Lednar's, which require action on the corporate level and are global in scope. In a factory or industrial setting, a medical director might spend the day meeting with employees individually and identifying solutions for their health problems. Such problems might include the concerns of a pregnant employee who is worried that her tasks could be injurious to the health of her unborn child, a machine-related laceration that needs care, or an employee who has had a heart attack, is in cardiac rehabilitation and needs help with a plan for his return to work. Factory medical directors deal with engineers about ergonomic interventions and work system design aspects to reduce musculoskeletal injuries, and can work with insurance companies if the need arises.

career at a glance

Wayne Lednar, MD, PhD

2002–Present	**Vice President and Director** Corporate Medical, Eastman Kodak Company, Rochester, N.Y.
1999–Present	**Adjunct Professor of Community and Occupational Medicine** State University of New York at Stony Brook
1995–Present	**Corporate Medical Director** Eastman Kodak Company
1991–Present	**Clinical Associate Professor of Toxicology** Department of Environmental Medicine, School of Medicine, University of Rochester
1988–Present	**Corporate Epidemiologist** Eastman Kodak Company
1988–Present	**Clinical Associate Professor** Community and Preventive Medicine, School of Medicine, University of Rochester
1992–1995	**Medical Director** Rochester Medical Services, Eastman Kodak Company
1984–1989	**Assistant Clinical Professor** Epidemiology, School of Public Health and Community Medicine and Member of the Graduate Faculty, University of Washington
1984–1988	**Director** Public Health Residency Program and **Assistant Chief** Preventive Medicine Service, Madigan Army Medical Center
1981–1988	**Adjunct Assistant Professor** Epidemiology, Uniformed Services University of the Health Sciences, Bethesda, MD
1981–1984	**Chief** Department of Advanced Preventive Medicine Studies **Director** General Preventive Medicine Residency Program, Walter Reed Army Institute of Research, Washington, D.C.
1976–1977	**Faculty Member** Department of Statistics, National Institutes of Health
1973–1976	**Research Associate** Department of Epidemiology and Occupational Health Studies Group, University of North Carolina

1 http:www.osha.gov/as/opa/osha-faq.html
2 Personal communication, Dr. Wayne Lednar, 1/11/02.
3 http://www.osha-slc.gov/OshDoc/data_General?Facts/jobsafetyandhealth-factsheet.htm

state environmentalist

State Environmentalist Checkpoint

Do you have a strong science background?

Are you willing to work with the business community, particularly planners and developers, to help maintain a safe environment for all?

Are you concerned about environmental problems and their effects on the health of populations?

If so, read on

A TRUE TALE

Thomas Burke, PhD, MPH, was raised in New Jersey. "As a kid growing up in that area in the '50s and '60s, you were really aware of your environment," he says. Those were times prior to environmental controls, when apartment house incinerators burned every night and there was very little regard for environmental protection. He recalls, "With the smokestacks cranking in the background, my friends and I would go swimming in the river. Sometimes we would leave on our undershirts and shorts, and we'd always get in trouble because our clothes would never be white again."

Thomas Burke, PhD, MPH

After graduating from St. Peter's College with a bachelor's degree in science, Dr. Burke went on to teach science to a class of "socially and educationally challenged children" in a high school in his hometown. The challenges of working with inner-city kids spurred his interest in public health and making a difference to the "big picture." It was enough to send him back to school to seek a master's in public health.

After receiving his MPH from the University of Texas, Dr. Burke served for ten years as Director of the Office of Science and Research in the New Jersey Department of Environmental Protection and as Assistant Commissioner for Occupational and Environmental Health. In 1986, Dr. Burke became New Jersey's Deputy Commissioner of Health. While working in New Jersey, he completed his doctorate in epidemiology at the University of Pennsylvania. Later, he was offered and seized the opportunity to become an Associate Professor at the Johns Hopkins

"One absolutely terrific thing about a career in environmental health is that it is never static. This tremendously evolving field presents constant new challenges. With sound scientific training, you can be working on the cutting edge of the nation's public health issues."

Bloomberg School of Public Health, where he focuses on environmental health science, epidemiology, risk assessment and public policy. Dr. Burke says he accepted the position because it allowed him to return to his first love, teaching.

Profiling the job

The major role of environmental health science (EHS) is to understand and identify those critical environmental exposures which may adversely impact human health. For someone who is interested in a career in the field, a strong science background is essential. Additionally, Dr. Burke says, an MPH can be a tremendous benefit because it provides a multidisciplinary foundation that allows people to be effective in management, epidemiology and biostatistics, and to bring a full kit of tools to any potential employer. An MPH also instills a broad problem-solving perspective, which is extremely important in this field.

The environmental health practitioner looking to subspecialize has many areas from which to choose. Toxicology is a good example of a busy subdiscipline. This subspecialty includes bench scientists, who perform laboratory experiments on animals to determine if certain environmental threats may cause harm to the public, and field scientists, who collect data in the field and perform environmental evaluation. In fall 2001, it was the field scientists who were on hand when the Hart Senate Office building was examined for anthrax. Field scientists also evaluate water supplies and research ways to avoid impacting the environment adversely.

Another popular area of this discipline is public policy, which offers an opportunity to fashion environmental legislation. "Environmental law is a large part of what we do," Dr. Burke says. One example of environmental law is The Clean Air Act, which creates a regulatory approach that allows the state or federal government to take control of a potentially harmful source of air pollution. The Clean Water Act operates similarly, and its enforcement allows people to drink water from almost any faucet in a public place with the assurance that the water is not contaminated. Dr. Burke initiated both these laws and was also personally involved in the shaping of the national Superfund, a law promoting the cleanup of hazardous waste sites, which gives states the resources to address toxic waste hazards in communities.

Did you know?
The average American home contains 3–10 gallons of hazardous materials.[1]

Did you know?
EPA studies
of human
exposure to
air pollutants
indicate that
indoor levels
of many pollu-
tants may be
2–5 times, and
occasionally,
more than 100
times higher
than outdoor
levels. Cleaning
products and
other house-
hold products
are among the
many culprits.[2]

Today, environmental health is being redefined with a view that the environment and the community are one and the same. Accordingly, environmental
health plays a role in community planning. On the state level, EHS faces
the challenge of addressing the balance between the needs of the business
community and commercial developers, and maintaining a safe environment.
On the local level, almost every community has specific environmental
problems, such as contaminated well fields and local factories that may pose
pollution problems. Many local environmental health issues fall outside
the reach of national environmental laws. "Interview local health officers,
and you get a very different perspective than you get in academia or in
Washington," says Dr. Burke. "Many of their concerns are very specific.
For example, rapid development has led to degraded water quality at our
bathing beaches, preventing swimming at these locations. We're losing these
critical community resources and it's a shame."

"Urban sprawl" is another current EHS concern. Although a clear definition
of sprawl remains elusive — some call it urban-like development outside of
central urban areas — the concern is that unrestricted and poorly planned
growth and low-density residential development threaten open spaces and
farmland, increase public service costs, send unnecessary networks of roads
cascading across once fertile fields and, most importantly, may degrade the
environment. With good land-use planning, however, EHS practitioners may
manage newly developed land so that urban development and growth
enhance the quality of life and at the same time protect the health of the
community's citizens.

A day in the life

Once a state environmentalist, Dr. Burke is now in academia. But, he is not
the typical academic environmentalist. Hopkins is an unusual place, where
he may regularly meet with the Department of Defense on terrorism issues
or the Department of Agriculture on food cultivation issues. He chairs the
advisory committee to the Director of Environmental Health at the Center
for Environmental Health, a position that keeps him directly involved in
national scientific challenges and the practical issues of environmental health.
He also works closely with the Centers for Disease Control and Prevention.

The most current issues of the field drive a typical day in the life of an environmental health scientist, with each day presenting fresh and varied tasks.

In fact, says Dr. Burke, the best aspect of environmental health practice is that there's never really a "typical day." Currently, he is working almost exclusively on addressing environmental health issues related to terrorism. "We have studies taking place at the World Trade Center to evaluate the health of the recovery workers at Ground Zero. We have conducted studies on the health of the firefighters who were there, and we are now looking at the recovery workers and the Teamsters still there." The safety of the postal system is a paramount concern, and his group is working assiduously on methods to sanitize the mail to prevent another anthrax situation.

"Unless we understand basic issues, such as the major public health challenges faced by a population or a community, public health doesn't work."

Thomas Burke, PhD, MPH

career at a glance

Thomas Burke, PhD, MPH

2002–Present	**Professor** Department of Health Policy and Management, Johns Hopkins Bloomberg School of Public Health
2001–Present	**Director** Johns Hopkins Bloomberg School of Public Health newly formed task force, Scientists Working to Address Terrorism (SWAT)
2000–Present	**Member** Institute of Medicine Panel, "Assuring the Health of the Public in the 21st Century"
1995–Present	**Founding Co-Director** Risk Sciences and Public Policy Institute, the Johns Hopkins University School of Hygiene and Public Health
1994–2002	**Associate Professor** Department of Health Policy and Management, the Johns Hopkins University School of Hygiene and Public Health
1990–1994	**Assistant Professor** Department of Health Policy and Management, the Johns Hopkins, University School of Hygiene and Public Health
1987–1990	**Deputy Commissioner** New Jersey Department of Health
1986–1987	**Assistant Commissioner** New Jersey Department of Health
1980–1986	**Director** Office of Science and Research, New Jersey Department of Environmental Protection
1977–1980	**Research Scientist** Office of Cancer and Toxic Substances Research, New Jersey Department of Environmental Protection
1976–1977	**Public Health Trainee** University of Texas, Health Science Center at Houston, School of Public Health
1974–1975	**Teacher of Health, Biology and Mathematics** Alternate High School, Patrick House Community Health Center

1 http://www.ems.org/household_cleaners/facts.html
2 http://www.ems.org/household_cleaners/facts.html

THE SANITARIAN IN PUBLIC HEALTH

"The environmentalist — also known as a sanitarian — is the key resource of environmental health," says William Parker, a registered professional environmentalist. Sanitarians serve as the public's guardians against unsafe and unhealthy environmental practices and conditions. In communities across the country, they work to ensure the safety and quality of air, water and food. These professionals are responsible for work in solid waste management, disease vector control and the handling and disposal of hazardous material. They play a vital role in environmental assessments, developing environmental policy and advocating for sound environmental health policies and practices.

As a sanitarian in the Environmental Sanitation Division of the Metropolitan Health Department in Nashville, Tennessee, Parker spends most of his time enforcing local and state health and sanitation codes on all private and public properties within the city. "I'm constantly dealing with situations of overgrown vegetation, illegal dumping and unsanitary conditions created by things like faulty plumbing that might possibly pollute our water supply. I also proactively seek out environmental problems and refer them to the proper environmentalists." Parker works closely with neighborhood organizations, governmental agencies outside his own department and elected officials to offer training sessions and strategy planning on issues of environmental health. He updates and develops environmental health codes in Memphis to keep them effective and current. "Investigating citizens' complaints of environmental problems is a challenging aspect of the job, but finding solutions, an even more challenging aspect of my work, is always extremely rewarding," Parker says.

A TRUE TALE

In 1949, when Richard Jackson, MD, MPH, was an infant, his 27-year-old father died of polio, leaving behind a very young wife and three children. "I truly believe," he says now, "that growing up after that personal tragedy motivated me to enter this field. The first merit badge I earned as a Boy Scout was in Public Health." Dr. Jackson's awareness of threats posed to the environment probably started in childhood. He grew up in New Jersey in the 1950s, a state known for its industrial base; his home was just a stone's throw from a polluted river. After graduating from St. Peter's College, Dr. Jackson attended Rutgers Medical School in New Jersey for two years. During the course of his training, the first autopsy he observed was of an ex-employee of an asbestos manufacturer. When the pathologist opened the man's abdomen, it looked like someone had filled it with plaster; the diagnosis was mesothelioma, an asbestos-related cancer. "I still remember that as he was doing the autopsy, the pathologist said to me: 'This is the third one of these I've seen this year. There must be something going on at a local plant.'"

Richard Jackson, MD, MPH

Because Rutgers was a two-year medical school, he transferred to the University of California at San Francisco (UCSF), graduated, and began a pediatric residency. Dr. Jackson took time off to work for the Centers for Disease Control and Prevention (CDC) as an officer in the Epidemic Intelligence Service (EIS), a two-year, postgraduate program of service and on-the-job training for health professionals interested in the practice of epidemiology. He says it was that experience that made him fall in love with public health. Assigned to New York as a state epidemiologist, Dr. Jackson found himself dealing firsthand with several now-infamous outbreaks of the mid-seventies: Legionnaire's disease, swine flu and Lyme disease. Right around that time he was detailed to India to work on smallpox eradication. Dr. Jackson traveled for three months in and around the border between India and Bangladesh, seeking but never finding a case of smallpox. "Near

Are you willing to be on the front lines, if necessary, in a disaster situation?

Do you enjoy working in the outdoors?

Would you be happy working in concert with many public health agencies — both in the United States and abroad?

If so, read on

eradication of the disease was exactly what everyone at the EIS hoped would happen," he says. "After that experience, I realized that I wanted to pursue a career in public health. I was hooked."

At the end of his EIS service, Dr. Jackson completed his pediatric residency, received an MPH from the University of California at Berkeley and went to work for the California Department of Health. Because he loved the outdoors, he was looking for a way to link his interest in the environment with his interest in human health and pediatrics, so it was no surprise that his first project addressed the health of children as affected by the environment.

In 1994, Dr. Jackson was named Director of the National Center for Environmental Health (NCEH), one of the centers within the CDC. Despite his numerous responsibilities, he is still a pediatrician at heart and has an ongoing and keen scientific interest in the public health effects of pesticides and other toxic substances, particularly as they may affect children. "It's a child's job to immerse herself in her environment," he says. "It's an absolutely normal part of human development that children taste, touch, smell and come into close contact with the world around them." His mission is to assure that that world is as safe as possible.

"At the NCEH, we are involved globally almost as much as we are domestically. No matter where and how we work, we are committed to safeguarding the health of the American public, both in the United States and abroad."

Profiling the job
Environmental health science is an interdisciplinary field that examines the ways in which biological, chemical and physical environmental agents affect human health. Environmental scientists work with government agencies, private organizations and community groups to identify and solve health problems. The field of EHS offers a broad selection of career opportunities that include risk assessment, waste management, engineering, ecological science, epidemiology and other biologically-oriented disciplines relating to the effects of the environment on humans. These effects are part of wider issues associated with water and air quality, sanitation, occupational safety and health, hazardous wastes, radiation and toxic substances.

A key mission of EHS is tracking the way a population's health is affected by the environment. In the past, information garnered from monitoring the physical environment — chemicals in the air, water and food — and information gathered from monitoring the health of the nation were isolated sets

of information. "The need to create a communications network that pulls this data together is urgent, so that people can actually see the impact of one subset on the other." Other disciplines need to be incorporated as well. People come into EHS from engineering, industrial hygiene, medicine, epidemiology and toxicology, to name just a few academic backgrounds. In some ways, it is a "big tent" that invites in many people not traditionally considered environmental health professionals, such as urban planners, architects, building and school designers and road builders. Yet, Dr. Jackson believes, they are all environmental health specialists in their own right, and their importance has to be recognized. "After all," he says, "how you design and build roads has as much to do with safety and air pollution as it does with moving people from place to place."

The NCEH, in particular, focuses on preventing illnesses that result from the interaction between populations and their environments. In addition to its primary environmental mission, the NCEH's public health responsibilities include prevention and treatment of birth defects and disabilities, laboratory science, and domestic and international emergencies. To implement its mission effectively, the NCEH works in partnership with numerous organizations and agencies, including federal, state and local health departments, environmental agencies, philanthropic foundations, and groups within industry and the community.

NCEH personnel consult, both globally and domestically, on humanitarian relief efforts for disasters such as war, hurricanes, earthquakes and floods, and technological disasters that include accidental releases into the atmosphere of radiation, chemical and biological agents.

Did you know?
Founded in 1951 by public health professor Alexander Langmuir, the Epidemic Intelligence Service (EIS) was first designed to act as an elite biological-warfare countermeasures unit of the Centers for Disease Control and Prevention (CDC).[1]

"Urban planners, architects, building and school designers, and road builders are all environmental health specialists in their own way, and we must recognize their importance. After all, how you design and build roads has as much to do with air pollution as it does with moving people from place to place."

Richard
Jackson,
MD, MPH

Children and the environment

Children's issues remain close to Dr. Jackson's heart. Many of the same environmental factors that affect adults affect children, he says, but they are more daunting to children. Because of a child's sensitivity, exposures early in life to substances such as lead, pesticides and mercury can adversely affect the development of both the body and brain, and might ultimately lead to reduced attention span, learning disabilities and behavior problems. These toxins have also been linked to lower IQs.[2]

"Fortunately, we're moving in the right direction with this problem," says Dr. Jackson, who recently completed, "The National Report on Human Exposure to Environmental Chemicals," the first comprehensive study of environmental chemicals in humans. In that study, through a collaborative effort of environmental, legal and public health professionals, blood and urine samples were obtained from 3,800 children and adults in 12 locations across the U.S., and screened for 27 chemicals. The results confirmed a continuing drop in lead levels nationwide, decreasing from more than 15 micrograms per deciliter in the 1970s[3] to less than 3 micrograms per deciliter today (any level over 10 micrograms per deciliter is elevated per CDC standards).

The continuous decline in blood-lead levels in children is good news for all age groups, says Dr. Jackson. "An emphasis on the reduction of environmental chemicals makes sense for all members of the population, even if they are at lesser direct risk than children. Children eat, drink and breathe three to four times as much per pound of body weight as do adults. Therefore, if you set an allowable pesticide level, or any toxin level, to protect a child, you end up protecting the entire population."

A day in the life

Dr. Jackson is familiar with the daily life of a public health professional from two perspectives. As an active research epidemiologist earlier in his career, he dealt head-on with major disease outbreaks. Currently, as Director of the NCEH, his primary responsibilities include policy formation, education and agency administration as well as direct engagement with public health initiatives.

"From where I sit, the medical practitioners who do best in public health are the ones who have excelled in a clinical setting," he says. "The skill sets that make you a good pediatrician, veterinarian or nurse are much the same as the attributes required for the public health profession — an ability to quickly size up a problem, come up with a potential solution, communicate with people, and zero in on the essential scientific, medical, clinical or psychological issues in a given situation."

As a research epidemiologist, Dr. Jackson would typically begin his day reviewing updates of disease surveillance reports or handling calls from the

public, media and elected officials. Some days might be largely devoted to the planning of studies related to a specific outbreak, such as a cluster of birth defects in an area with contaminated water. "In those cases, I'd work with fellow researchers or practicing physicians, or perhaps environmental specialists and field staff to develop and test questionnaires in the field." Often the data yielded by these questionnaires would form the basis of a policy directive or departmental public statement. "The bigger the issue, the more time it takes, the more people it involves, the more talk it generates and the more research it requires to move something forward and generate some kind of public benefit," Dr. Jackson notes.

As Director of the NCEH, Dr. Jackson works about 60 hours a week, by his own estimate. Consider his account of a recent day: "In the morning, I opened a meeting of invited experts grappling with the question of how to prepare for nuclear and radiologic terrorism. In the afternoon I attended a seminar presented by two of our staff members who have been working in Afghani refugee camps, overseeing nutritional assessments, cause-of-death assessments, and immunization efforts. Afterwards, I spoke to a group about reshaping our physical environments to reduce pollution and promote exercise and physical activity."

Though based in Atlanta, Dr. Jackson is generally in Washington one day a week, working with HHS officials, or agencies such as the Environmental Protection Agency (EPA) and National Institutes of Health (NIH), environmental advocacy groups, and legislators. Meetings with a state health

department or university might take up another day. He also travels frequently, giving lectures and presentations throughout the country.

On a visit to New Mexico, Dr. Jackson met with state university students and professors to discuss local CDC instruction programs for students from disadvantaged communities. "There are real health disparities in our population and CDC is very committed to increasing the numbers of minorities, in this case Hispanics and Native Americans, in public health," he says. He then met with the formal advisory board of the School of Public Health to discuss general public health issues, funding, training, and terrorism response. The next morning he delivered the plenary address at a meeting of the New Mexico Public Health Association.

"I'm lucky enough to have a job where I can use all my training," he says. "This is highly multidisciplinary work which includes epidemiology, toxicology, medicine, chemistry, mathematics, political science, communication and public speaking and — the most challenging and gratifying of all — management of other people. I love to learn, and I find that nothing I learn ever goes to waste."

career at a glance <<<

Richard Jackson, MD, MPH

2000–Present	**Adjunct Professor** Department of Environmental & Occupational Health, The George Washington University
1998–Present	**Adjunct Professor** Department of Environmental & Occupational Health, Rollins School of Public Health, Emory University
1994–Present	**Director** National Center for Environmental Health, Centers for Disease Control and Prevention
1986–Present	**Assistant Clinical Professor** Department of Medicine University of California, San Francisco
1992–1994	**Chief** Division of Communicable Disease Control, California State Department of Health Service
1991–1992	**Chief** Hazard Identification and Risk Assessment Branch, Office of Environmental Health Hazard Assessment, Public Health Administrator I, California Environmental Protection Agency
1990–1991	**Chief** Hazard Identification and Risk Assessment Branch, Public Health Medical Officer III, California State Department of Health Services
1988–1990	**Acting Chief** Office of Environmental Health Hazard Assessment, Public Health Medical Officer III, California State Department of Health Services
1985–1988	**Chief** Hazard Evaluation Section, Public Health Medical Officer III, California State Department of Health Services
1985–1986	**Acting Chief** California Occupational Health Program, Public Health Medical Officer III, California State Department of Health Services
1982–1985	**Chief** Community Toxicology Unit, Public Health Medical Officer II, Services, Epidemiological Studies Section, California State Department of Health Services
1979–1982	**Chief** Pesticide Unit, Public Health Medical Officer II, Medical Epidemiologist, Epidemiological Studies Section, California State Department of Health Services
1975–1977	**Epidemic Intelligence Service (EIS) Officer** U.S. Public Health Service, Centers for Disease Control and Prevention
1976	**Special Epidemiologist** World Health Organization, Smallpox Eradication Program

1 http://www.cdcfoundation.org/eis/
2 http://www.childenvironment.org/reports/tty_2000-05-02_hr.htm
3 http://epbiwww.cwru.edu/mmwr/vol46/mm4607.html#article1

public health preparedness

By William
Roper, MD,
MPH, Dean,
School of
Public Health,
University of
North Carolina
at Chapel Hill

The average American understands what a medical school is, what a nurse and pharmacist do and what hospitals are for. But for most people, the who and the what of public health is a largely unknown territory.

The one constant in my public health career — which over the years has taken me from the local level to state and federal government, into the private sector, and now academia — has been the chorus of people who ask, "Tell me again, what is it that you do?" An extraordinary question, when one considers that almost every person in the United States has had their life touched by public health professionals and practices. Ironically, public health has not been readily seen as relevant to the daily lives of most of the very people we serve.

William Roper, MD, MPH

Sadly, in the aftermath of the autumn of 2001, explaining my work has become considerably easier. Although public health is much more than preparedness, today it is that aspect of the field that is foremost in people's minds. The current relevance of public health to national security has made it easier to explain: "Public health is what's on the news tonight, and it's what you will read in *The New York Times* tomorrow morning. It's chlorine dioxide in the Hart Senate Building and electromagnetic mail sanitizers. It's ensuring the country has an adequate stockpile of smallpox vaccine." All at once, everyone gets it, or at least part of it.

While public health preparedness may be the topic of the moment, it is certainly not a new concept. But it took the events of September 11, the anthrax threat and the fear of biological weapons to give the general public a reason to be concerned and to catapult the topic to the forefront of national discussion. It is gratifying to hear people in positions of leadership simply use the phrase "public health preparedness." From the President of the United States to the Secretary of the Department of Homeland Security, to senators and congressmen, to governors and mayors, influential eyes have been opened to the importance of public health. And increasingly, the voting public is *insisting* on spending substantial amounts of federal, state and local money to ensure the highest level of public health preparedness possible.

In the early '70s, many respected and influential health professionals proclaimed that the era of infectious disease was over and that we should turn our attention to chronic non-communicable diseases and injury control.[1] We have learned, much to our regret, that the problems of infectious diseases have not gone away. They have simply adapted and evolved with the global community, continuing to threaten us as much — in some ways even more — than ever.

Despite the newness of the terrorist threat, we saw a spectacularly professional and integrated response to the attacks of 2001. Immediately after September 11 – well before the first case of inhalation anthrax was confirmed on October 4 — the CDC instituted a nationwide health alert system, putting state and local health departments and 81 laboratories across the country on high alert for people presenting any inexplicable or puzzling symptoms of any kind. By the morning of September 12, the CDC had a team of 35 epidemiologists in New York. In addition to the professionals, 50 tons of medical supplies also arrived in New York within seven hours of the aircraft attack. The existing National Disaster Medical System activated many of its 7,000 at-the-ready medical professionals and dispatched five Disaster Medical Assistance Teams to New York and three to Washington, also within 24 hours.[2]

This kind of response demonstrates that we are far more prepared for infectious outbreaks than many critics have suggested. At the same time, it is also true that we are far less prepared than many of us in the field desire.

In 1993, alarmed by a disturbing number of his patients showing unusual symptoms, an alert pediatric gastroenterologist prevented an *E. coli* catastrophe in the Pacific Northwest when he warned the Washington State Department of Health of a potential major outbreak. Within a week, the department had traced the infection to hamburgers at a fast food chain.[3] While many people were infected, and several patients lost their lives, the spread of the deadly food was halted, and a much greater tragedy prevented. The incident was a testament to the high value of up-to-date knowledge and maximum attentiveness in front-line practitioners, and to the necessity of good lines of communication and the ability for regional health departments to deploy a rapid response.

When you stop and think about it, the threat of bioterrorism is not all that different from the threat posed by tainted hamburgers. Once again, professionals on the front lines — physicians, nurses, pharmacists, emergency technicians and ambulance personnel — stay alert for anything unusual to report to their county, state and federal public health authorities. Effective surveillance is always the first line of public health defense.

Once an outbreak is identified, natural or deliberate in origin, response is the next critical phase. Our facilities and capabilities for medical response at the local, first-responder level are strong, and we are working to make them stronger. Federal and state agencies are continuing to coordinate with local health departments for emergency response. The public health system is providing physicians and other medical professionals with continuing education and training. The CDC is also expanding the number of positions in the Epidemic Intelligence Service, a department essential to managing the process.

We are accelerating our research on infectious agents, enhancing our current laboratory methods for identifying them, and producing more and new vaccines and antibiotics. As the *E. coli* example demonstrates, protection of our food and water supply is also of paramount concern. Even without the threat of bioterrorism, there is the possibility of contaminants entering our food or water at nearly every point in its source, production and distribution. Thus active and continuous coordination between the public health infrastructure, and the food service industry and municipalities with reservoir responsibilities, is more essential than ever before.

Dry runs and drills can also help test our preparedness and assist us in refining old responses and creating new ones. In the winter of 2002, four organizations — the Center for Strategic and International Studies, the Johns Hopkins Center for Civilian Biodefense Studies, the ANSER Institute for Homeland Security, and the Oklahoma City National Memorial Institute for the Prevention of Terrorism — collaborated on a bioterrorism exercise named "Dark Winter," which simulated a possible reaction to a deliberate release of aerosolized smallpox in the United States. The scenario, conducted at Andrews Air Force Base in Washington, D.C., was played out over three successive mock National Security Council meetings, in which former senior government officials took on the roles of NSC members. Over the thirteen days of the exercise, the participants reached several conclusions: the current public health infrastructure, especially in its organizational/communications structure, is still not adequate for the task of dealing with such a deliberate attack; our ability to handle both a suddenly high number of infected patients and to vaccinate those not infected, also known as "surge capability," is insufficient; and information management and control would be critical to handling the outbreak. While these conclusions underscore the need to make changes, there is no other country better equipped to face what is both a domestic and global health threat. Many public health careers will be made as we take on this threat — the time is ripe, and the need is urgent.

Strengthening the nation's public health infrastructure goes well beyond the need to be prepared for chemical or bioterrorism. The same tools will be of great value in identifying, tracking and treating naturally occurring infectious diseases. Much of what we learn will be applicable to other kinds of disasters, including natural disasters such as floods, hurricanes and earthquakes. We are settling for nothing less than being at-the-ready with well-trained personnel, state-of-the-art communications capabilities, analytical resources and treatments.

Preparedness is everyone's job. As such, it must include a readiness among public health professionals to take on new and unexpected tasks, not always within their zones of comfort. Physicians, for example, need to expand their roles. When dealing with infectious outbreaks, they will need to assume the epidemiologist's role, and think in terms of vectors, numbers, locations and causes. Conversely, epidemiologists, pharmacists, and nurses in public health should cross-train wherever possible to be able to assist with direct medical care in emergency situations.

Preparedness is not only about taking on the duties you were trained to take on and those you were not, preparedness is also about awareness and maintaining an alert posture in daily life, on and off the job. Put most simply, public health professionals have to be ready, willing and able to act at the very first telephone call. The potential to be called to service at any time to be part of a mobilization effort is part of what makes this career so vital. Another part is the opportunity to be a leader when necessary.

Leaders must be team players able to work with first responder counterparts among police, firefighters and military personnel. We must develop and maintain our networks of communication with our partners throughout the nation, indeed throughout the world. Most of you reading this will already be familiar with and educated in the core competencies essential to being good public health leaders, such as training in teamwork, communications and tactical decision making. Perhaps all you will lack is the direct experience. These challenging times promise unprecedented opportunities for gaining new experience. Seize them.

Tragic events have drawn intense attention to the nation's public health infrastructure. Whether we'll see a waning of that intensity depends partly on situations well beyond our control, but partly on the commitment and action of all public health professionals. I'd like to believe that serious people, whether they are presidents, governors, mayors or journalists, will recall our level of public health indifference on September 10, 2001. We can't go back there again. Public health needs the attention and long overdue funding that appears to be coming our way. We need to make sure that both the government and the public maintain the current sense of urgency surrounding public health. Why? Because our lives depend on it.

William Roper, MD, MPH is Dean of the School of Public Health at the University of North Carolina at Chapel Hill (UNC). He also is Professor of Health Policy and Administration in the School of Public Health and is Professor of Pediatrics in the School of Medicine at UNC. Prior to joining UNC in July 1997, Dr. Roper was Senior Vice-President of Prudential Health Care. Before going to Prudential, Dr. Roper was Director of the Centers for Disease Control and Prevention, served on the senior White House staff, and was administrator of the Health Care Financing Administration. He received his medical degree from the University of Alabama School of Medicine, and his master's in public health from the University of Alabama at Birmingham School of Public Health. Dr. Roper is a member of the Institute of Medicine of the National Academy of Sciences and serves on the Institute of Medicine governing council.

1 http://www.abc.net.au/science/slab/antibiotics/history.htm
2 http://www.advanceforaud.com/previousdnw/aadnw0910.html
3 http://www.doh.wa.gov/topics/ecoli.htm

A TRUE TALE

At the conclusion of his first year of medical school at the University of Rochester, Dale Morse, MD, MS, spent the summer on a Navajo Indian reservation investigating disease patterns. He enjoyed epidemiology so much

Dale L. Morse, MD, MS

that as a fourth year medical student he set up his own four-week elective at a county health department "just to see what people in public health do." Serendipitously, he happened to be there when two important health issues emerged. The first was a small outbreak of an allergic reaction among children to a dye in popular "tattoos" they bought. The second was a huge community outbreak of giardiasis, a gastrointestinal illness caused by a parasite found in water. The giardiasis outbreak was so serious that a team from the Centers for Disease Control and Prevention (CDC) came up from Atlanta to investigate. The Epidemic Intelligence Service (EIS) officer on the scene asked Dr. Morse if he wanted to help with the investigation. After that experience, he knew he would be an epidemiologist.

After graduating from medical school, Dr. Morse interned in internal medicine, and then joined the CDC as an EIS officer. Upon completing his residency, he joined the New York State Department of Health. Except for "sabbaticals" at Harvard to earn his master's in epidemiology, and a year as a consultant for the British government at their communicable disease surveillance center in London, he spent the next 20 years at the New York State Department of Health as an epidemiologist, rising through the ranks from Assistant Bureau Director to Director of Infectious Disease, to his current position as Director, Office of Science and Public Health.

"Working through a disaster is like transitioning from working on a general medical floor to a busy hospital emergency room. You're doing some of the same things you might do in your routine as an epidemiologist, but everything is intensely time-driven."

State Epidemiologist Checkpoint

Do you enjoy solving difficult and involved puzzles?

Would you find it exciting to track down the cause of infectious disease outbreaks?

Would you enjoy the challenge of working through a public health disaster?

If so, read on

Profiling the job

Epidemiology and surveillance programs provide the scientific foundation for public health. Dr. Morse suggests that this profession can best be approached with a medical degree or through training at a school of public health, although some people work their way up by starting as sanitarians, for example, or as nurses in local health departments.

Over the span of a career, an infectious disease epidemiologist will investigate many different types of outbreaks. These might be food borne, such as the outbreaks in New York State in 1982 of gastroenteritis and hepatitis associated with the consumption of raw clams, and food-borne typhoid and listeria. Other outbreaks are transmitted by direct contact, such as the case clusters of meningococcal meningitis Dr. Morse has witnessed on college campuses and in school districts, where thousands of doses of vaccine were administered to prevent secondary cases.

In these instances, epidemiological methods must be applied and activities among multiple public health groups must be coordinated. At the local level, those involved include the commissioner of health, public health nurses, sanitarians and environmental specialists. At the state level, activities are coordinated among laboratory epidemiologists, biostatisticians, public affairs groups, environmental scientists and those who oversee health care services. At the federal level, the CDC's experts are often recruited, as are personnel from the Food and Drug Administration (FDA), United States Drug Administration (USDA), Environmental Protection Agency (EPA), National Institutes of Health (NIH) and other organizations.

Two high-profile public health crises Dr. Morse has worked on were the West Nile virus outbreak and the bioterrorist use of anthrax. When the initial West Nile virus case was reported in 1999, Dr. Morse was working in Albany at the Wadsworth Center laboratories of the New York State Department of Health. The outbreak was unprecedented, he says. The virus, which is transmitted by mosquitoes and carried in birds, had never before been seen in the Western Hemisphere.

Dr. Morse believes that credit for the initial detection of the virus should go to a New York City physician who reported the first two cases of unusual illness in patients, and to the New York City Health Department officials who investigated those cases. The physician assumed her patients had encephalitis, but noted uncharacteristic muscle weakness, which prompted her to call the City Health Department. The New York City Health Department sent two physicians to interview the initial group of patients. When similar cases arose, the department mounted a full-blown investigation. Specimens were sent to Wadsworth for testing, and Wadsworth scientists who noted antibodies to St. Louis encephalitis (SLE) in the blood samples made this initial diagnosis.

After the CDC confirmed the diagnosis of SLE, the Health Department instituted measures to control mosquitoes and reduce the public's exposure. Several weeks later, however, several epidemiologists noted unusual aspects of the outbreak that a diagnosis of SLE couldn't alone explain. For example, birds in the city had been dying in numbers larger than usual, although these deaths had not at first been recognized as part of the outbreak. SLE literature did not suggest that SLE killed birds at all. Additionally, the titers in some patients were not as high as they should have been for cases of St. Louis encephalitis. Finally, some of the tests done on the patients' spinal fluid in the molecular laboratory showed no evidence of SLE. The connection between birds and humans was made only after some of the bird autopsies showed a form of encephalitis similar to that being found in the humans. The identical West Nile encephalitis virus (WNV) was identified in both human and avian populations.[2]

Dr. Morse outlines the steps taken in an outbreak investigation as follows:

○ Check validity of information received;

○ Verify the diagnosis;

○ Search for additional cases to determine whether there is an outbreak;

○ Establish clear definition of the disease (case definition);

○ Make arrangements for laboratory support;

○ Verify the diagnosis of potential secondary cases;

○ Characterize each case in terms of time, place and person (case finding);

Did you know?
The Centers for Disease Control and Prevention estimates that the release of 100 kilograms of aerosolized anthrax would result in approximately 130,000 to three million deaths and would carry an estimated economic burden of $26.2 billion per 100,000 people exposed to the spores.[1]

○   Hypothesize what is causing the outbreak or identify the source;

○   Develop analytic studies to try to ascertain whether the hypothesis is correct;

○   Conduct control measures; and

○   Inform the public.[3]

"No one is an island anymore," says Dr. Morse. "Treatment and containment of an illness such as that caused by West Nile virus requires the expertise of a number of people." This particular investigation included the expertise of epidemiologists, entomologists, veterinarians, zoo directors, national wildlife groups, academic centers and lab technicians. The investigation's success was due in large part to the rapid communication with the laboratory, where Wadsworth scientists were in contact with the epidemiologists and environmental groups at least twice a day. In addition, local and state health departments communicated openly with the CDC. "We had conference calls twice a day, in which up-to-the-minute information was presented to all groups working on the outbreak, so that they could then determine their next steps. We also set up a computerized health information network that connected local health departments with state health departments. That network allowed us to instantly share case reports, public announcements, press releases and scientific articles. In the end, there were 62 confirmed cases of West Nile and seven deaths in the New York area, but we prevented what could have been a far greater disaster."

The anthrax attack that occurred in 2001, another high profile case, was similar to dealing with other emerging infections, Morse says. Although the number of cases was small, the level of concern was and continues to be very high because anthrax fits the profile of "dreaded disease phenomena," i.e. illnesses that might be rare but are extremely severe in their impact. When anthrax was diagnosed in the first patient, the laboratory used the tools gathered from previous disease outbreaks. "The investigation required all the same correspondence and communication components that we had developed in our West Nile experience," Dr. Morse says. In the end, the laboratory had to gear up to test large numbers of specimens and develop new capabilities very rapidly. "This was particularly difficult," he notes, "for something that really hadn't been handled before, at least environmentally."

A day in the life

Epidemiologists are sometimes referred to as "medical detectives," says Dr. Morse. "They're responsible for tracking and analyzing patterns of health and disease with the goal of improving the overall health of the population." Indeed, unraveling the mysteries behind disease outbreaks and patterns of conditions is a key part of the epidemiologist's role.

"This can be a fast-moving and extremely challenging profession," Dr. Morse says. He compares working through an outbreak and an "everyday" disease-state cluster or pattern investigation to the difference between working on a general medical floor and working in an emergency room. "Basically," he says, "you are doing some of the same things you might do in your routine

life as an epidemiologist, but everything is intensely time-driven. You're faced with high pressure and an accelerated need to respond quickly. You don't have time to reflect."

In an outbreak, the epidemiologist's role includes zeroing in on a diagnosis and looking for additional cases to verify whether in fact an outbreak exists. "We then make a hypothesis

as to the cause of the outbreak and develop analytic studies to determine whether our hypothesis is correct. We also conduct control measures and make sure to keep the public and professional community current on what's happening."

As epidemiologist and Director of the Office of Science and Public Health, Dr. Morse coordinates activities among the New York State Health Department Centers for Epidemiology, Laboratory and Environmental Services. He is also responsible for overseeing scientific epidemiologic investigations and serves as either principal or co-principal investigator on a number of studies, including those on emerging infections, a bioterrorism grant, an asthma grant and several communicable diseases.

"My work crosses many disciplines, centers and regions," he notes "and my job is to coordinate among them — via phone, e-mail and in-person meetings that typically involve people from the various sections of my department as well as other divisions in the State Department of Health." In a sense, he says, "epidemiology at the local and state — rather than federal — level offers more of an opportunity to work on the front lines of public health. It's really where science and practice come together."

>> **career at a glance**

Dale L. Morse, MD, MS	
2001–Present	**Director** Office of Science and Public Health, New York State Department of Health
2000–Present	**Professor of Medicine** Albany Medical College
1995–Present	**Full Professor** Department of Epidemiology, School of Public Health, State University of New York at Albany
1997–2001	**Director** Division of Infectious Disease, and Director for Epidemiology, Wadsworth Center for Laboratories and Research, New York State Department of Health
1996–1997	**Director for Epidemiology** Wadsworth Center for Laboratories and Research, New York State Department of Health
1993–1997	**Chair** Department of Epidemiology, School of Public Health, State University of New York at Albany
1993–1996	**Director** Division of Epidemiology, New York State Department of Health
1985–1996	**State Epidemiologist** New York State Department of Health
1987–1994	**Associate Professor** Department of Epidemiology, School of Public Health, State University of New York at Albany
1992–1993	**Head** Field Services Unit, Communicable Disease Surveillance Center, Public Health Laboratory Service, London, England
1982–1993	**Director** Bureau of Communicable Disease Control, New York State Health Department
1980–1982	**Assistant Director** Bureau of Disease Control, New York State Health Department
1976–1978	**Epidemic Intelligence Service Officer** Centers for Disease Control and Prevention

1 http://www.hopkins-biodefense.org/pages/agents/agentanthrax.html
2 http://www.aphis.usda.gov/vs/ep/WNV/summary.html
3 Personal communication, Dr. Dale Morse, 1/16/02.

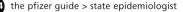

A TRUE TALE

Lawrence Sturman, MD, PhD, never dreamed he would be spending almost his entire career in a public health laboratory. After receiving his medical degree from Northwestern University Medical School and completing a year of clinical training at the Hospital of the University of Pennsylvania, he realized his interests ran toward research. To that end, Dr. Sturman attended The Rockefeller University, where he earned a doctorate in virology. He spent the following two years at the National Institutes of Health Laboratory of Viral Diseases. There he met a fellow virologist who invited him to visit the Wadsworth Center in Albany, New York, then known as the Division of Laboratories and Research of the New York State Department of Health. He was told the organization was "a cross between a mini-NIH and a mini-CDC." Dr. Sturman agreed to take a position at Wadsworth, but assumed it would be for a short time. "Certainly not for 30 years!" he says. In 1989, Dr. Sturman became Director of the Wadsworth Center's Division of Clinical Sciences, and in 1992 he was appointed Director of the Wadsworth Center.

Lawrence S. Sturman, MD, PhD

Laboratory Director Checkpoint

Do you enjoy science and have the ability to work with precision?

Do you like learning and applying new knowledge to different issues?

Does making a difference matter to you?

Do you work well as a member of a team?

If so, read on

"Today, public health preparedness in the laboratory means having the facilities, the people and the knowledge to deal rapidly with any health matters as they arise — be they environmental issues, infectious diseases or considerations of genetics."

Profiling the job

The Wadsworth Center, which has 1,100 employees and is a part of the New York State Department of Health, is the largest and most comprehensive state public health laboratory in the nation. Established in 1901 as the State Antitoxin Laboratory, it was first known for producing high quality biological products, such as diphtheria antitoxin.[1] Today, Wadsworth remains committed to responding to public health threats by developing and applying advanced technologies.

Such technologies have had a dramatic impact on the definition of preparedness. "When I think of public health preparedness," Dr. Sturman says, "I realize that what would have constituted preparedness from the laboratory standpoint in 1950 or even 1980 is not what we need today. Today, public health preparedness in the lab means having the facilities, the people and the knowledge to deal rapidly with any health matters as they arise, whether they are environmental issues, infectious diseases or considerations of genetics. We depend very much on the knowledge base of our staff. They are our intellectual capital."

That intellectual capital was brought to bear on a critical public health issue in late 2001. The Wadsworth Center became involved to a large degree in the anthrax situation and was well prepared for it. "Back in 1999," Dr. Sturman says, "an FBI agent telephoned us, saying that they had an anthrax threat letter in Vermont, and requested that Wadsworth test the letter. That event turned out to be a fortunate spur to the development of anthrax-specific preparedness. When this latest situation came along, we had a core of people who were trained, and we had the proper methods for testing already in place. We had laboratory protocols, we had molecular tests and we had a method for determining whether spores of the deadly bacteria were present." What Wadsworth Center did not have was the capability to handle the volume of requests for testing that started coming into the laboratory in late 2001.

Dr. Sturman asked for volunteers from the microbiology laboratory to supplement the existing bioterrorism team, eight individuals specially trained in handling pathogenic and potentially lethal agents. An expanded group of 30 Wadsworth scientists worked in a Biosafety Level Three (BSL-3) facility, where they were required to wear protective suits and face masks. Testing was carried out 24 hours a day. The State Emergency Management Office was involved, as were the FBI and the state police, and a protocol was developed for handling and processing samples as they arrived. Nearly 1,000 environmental samples had been tested by the end of the year 2001. Twenty-four samples tested positive for anthrax, among them samples from several media outlets.

Whether the next public health crisis comes from a bioterrorist threat or a newly emerged pathogen such as West Nile virus, Wadsworth Center's unique characteristic as a research-intensive public health laboratory provides the expertise needed to respond. There are organic chemists, atmospheric chemists, and a wide range of microbiologists, virologists, parasitologists and other specialists. There are also research scientists in rapidly evolving fields such as genomics, bioinformatics and nanobiotechnology. They are specialists who can provide informed answers when called upon — but need not necessarily have formal public health degrees or training. Although Wadsworth is a public health laboratory, Dr. Sturman says an MPH is not a requisite to success there. Some who work in public health laboratories have

bachelor's degrees, master's degrees, or medical technology training. A degree in science is preferred, he says.

"Other state public health laboratories may not conduct the kind of research activities that take place at Wadsworth," Dr. Sturman explains, "but Wadsworth in turn does not perform functions that some other public health laboratories do. Ours is a reference laboratory. We perform complex tests not available elsewhere, as well as confirmatory tests. While some public health laboratories carry out a high volume of routine tests — they may do hundreds of thousands of

syphilis serologies, for example — we perform large numbers of routine tests only if there happens to be an outbreak or a special need." For example, all state laboratories routinely monitor drinking water, but Wadsworth tests drinking water principally if there is a complaint or a problem in an area, or if requested by a local health department. They also provide specialized testing not widely available elsewhere, such as for *Cryptosporidium*.

Wadsworth does perform some high-volume laboratory services, including newborn screening for such metabolic disorders as phenylketonuria, branch chain ketonuria and galactosemia, for every baby born in New York State. With the State averaging more than 250,000 annual births, this is Wadsworth's highest-volume laboratory service by far. Wadsworth also conducts hundreds of thousands of HIV tests each year. The arbovirus program has been regularly testing large numbers of mosquitoes, birds, and other animals for West Nile virus since the virus made its first North American appearance in New York State in 1999.

The laboratory also safeguards the health of the public by providing certification for all clinical and environmental laboratories that test specimens originating in New York State. "One of our top responsibilities is laboratory quality certification. We supply the materials and the experience so that we can certify other laboratories to accurately perform and report tests," says Dr. Sturman. A team of specialists inspects each laboratory, administers proficiency tests and reviews the qualifications of the staff and their methodologies. Wadsworth staff members also oversee blood and tissue banks statewide.

A day in the life

Solitude plays little part in Dr. Sturman's daily schedule, which is a continual sequence of interactions with staff, colleagues, biomedical luminaries and others. He begins one recent workday joining the State Health Commissioner on morning rounds, then moving on to discuss a disease outbreak in upstate New York. A meeting with his counterparts in the Heath Department's Center for Environmental Health and Center for Community Health follows. The subject is testing procedures for infectious diseases.

Late that morning, he confers with a Wadsworth administrator about grant programs that fund breast cancer and spinal cord injury research, leaving his office at noon to have lunch with the director of a joint Wadsworth-Albany Medical College research program aimed at rapidly moving laboratory discoveries to clinical application.

Back in his office, Dr. Sturman prepares for a visit the next day by a Nobel Prize-winning scientist, who has been invited to deliver the Department of Health's Centennial Lecture. Needing an update from the West Nile virus team he assembled after the initial outbreak in New York State, Dr. Sturman drives to Wadsworth's arbovirus laboratory, housed at a 200-acre farm in a community just outside Albany. His last meeting of the day is at another Wadsworth facility back in Albany, where he talks with other scientists about progress on specific infectious disease protocols.

The daily life of a public health laboratorian is no less busy than Dr. Sturman's, but clearly follows a different track. Drawing upon research methods used in public health and health sciences research, laboratorians perform a wide range of tasks. A typical morning might find a laboratory specialist performing genetic assays on parents concerned about being Tay-Sachs carriers, having earlier spent time developing and applying quality assurance criteria for those assays. Then she might conduct follow-up tests on blood samples.

In the afternoon, the public health laboratorian might move from lab to community, perhaps leading a training seminar on sterile technique for biology teachers at a local high school, or discussing standard laboratory practices with technicians in a police department's forensics lab. Towards the end of the day, she might attend a seminar at a nearby research institution. Altogether, a public health laboratorian is a busy worker in a widely varied field that blends hard science, interaction with a variety of publics, and the desire to make a difference.

career at a glance

Lawrence S. Sturman, MD, PhD

1995–Present	**Professor** Department of Biomedical Sciences, School of Public Health, The University at Albany, State University of New York
1992–Present	**Director** Wadsworth Center, New York State Department of Health, Albany, N.Y.
1985–1995	**Chair** Department of Biomedical Sciences, School of Public Health, The University at Albany, State University of New York
1989–1991	**Director** Division of Clinical Sciences, Wadsworth Center
1970–1989	**Research Physician** Laboratory of Virology, Wadsworth Center
1968–1970	**Staff Associate and Surgeon** Laboratory of Viral Disease, National Institute of Allergy and Infectious Disease, National Institutes of Health

1 www.health.state.ny.us/nysdoh/commish/history/historical_timeline.htm

public health lawyer

A TRUE TALE

Lawrence Gostin's path into public health took him from North Carolina to the U.K., to Sicily, to Cambridge and finally to Washington. It began in law school and continues today with academic affiliations. Along the way, a combination of personalities, passion and a deadly epidemic guided him into his career.

Lawrence O. Gostin, JD, LLD (Hon.)

After graduating from Duke Law School, Gostin, JD, LLD (Hon.) went directly to Oxford University on a Fulbright scholarship. He remained in England for 11 years, working as a Legal Director of the National Association for Mental Health and as a faculty member at Oxford University. Then while he was attending a meeting in Sicily he met Dr. William Curran who, at the time, was Professor of Health Law at Harvard University. Dr. Curran convinced him to come to Harvard as an NIH Fellow and to accept a position as adjunct professor of public health and law. While at Harvard, Gostin also became the Executive Director of the American Society of Law, Medicine, & Ethics.

Gostin cites two studies he led in the early 80s concerned with the then new AIDS epidemic as critical factors in shaping his career: the U.S. AIDS Litigation Project and the Harvard Model AIDS Legislation Project. It was these studies, Gostin says, conducted in the early and baffling first years of the HIV crisis, that confirmed his interest in public health.

In 1995, Gostin received an offer to consider a joint position as Professor of Law at Georgetown University and Professor of Public Health at Johns Hopkins University. The appointment was part of a unique program combining law and public health, known as the Center for Law and the Public's Health (CLPH) at Johns Hopkins and Georgetown Universities. CLPH was founded with

"Public health authorities require certain legal powers to be effective, but, at the same time, they must continue to respect individual rights and show toleration of groups."

support from the Centers for Disease Control and Prevention (CDC), and serves as a primary national resource on public health law, ethics and policy for public health practitioners, lawyers, legislators, policymakers and others. Gostin is presently the center's director.

Profiling the job

Public health lawyers work in an area of law that has wide-ranging effects on American life. They are involved in policy, regulation and legislation that governs public health-related activities, such as municipal spraying of pesticides to wipe out mosquito concentrations or determining acceptable levels of natural toxins in water reservoirs. When enforced, public health laws are among the most potent tools available for promoting health and preserving life. Think of the seat belt laws that were enacted around the nation in the late '80s and early '90s. "These laws are critical to the public health system because they promote a kind of health education and method of changing health-related behavior," says Gostin.

Significant constitutional issues often come into play in the world of public health law. For example, where medical interventions may become illegally compulsory, public health lawyers are charged with protecting an individual's rights to due process. When dealing with the possibility of potentially infectious outbreaks, public health lawyers need to strike a balance between the sensitive issue of individual privacy and the public's need to know.

Another area of responsibility for public health lawyers involves managing lawsuits on behalf of the state against any facility or company that may be in violation of state health regulations. They also participate in the approval process for licensing and regulating all health care personnel. Public health lawyers are often called upon to manage the guardianship of hospitalized people who may not be competent to represent themselves. Perhaps the public health lawyer's most far-reaching task is to advise legislators on constructing new health laws and writing and adjudicating agency procedures for implementing and enforcing the law.

Today, lawyers interested in a career in public health law have unlimited opportunities. Virtually every category of law has some public health application. Lawyers can work in local, state or national public health agencies with wide oversight and policy responsibilities. The health divisions of law firms have commercial opportunities, and hundreds of volunteer and social

"In whatever way you practice, public health law is an exciting and rewarding place to be."

Lawrence Gostin, JD, LLD (Hon.)

action organizations have opportunities for not-for-profit work. Those interested in contract law will negotiate, develop, comply with and cancel contracts with other persons, organizations and agencies for the provision of essential public health services. Lawyers practicing general public health law can expect to become involved in all essential facets of assuring the public's health, including imposing quarantines, revoking or suspending business and medical licenses, monitoring confidentiality in the collection or release of medical data, mandatory institutionalizations and closings of unsafe public premises.

"People entering the field need to be sure they understand the difference between health care law and public health law," says Gostin. He explains

the difference this way: *health care law* primarily deals with regulating medical practice and personal health care, and mandating and regulating the health care delivery system, its financing, and conducting research. *Public health* law, on the other hand, is primarily concerned with the government's powers and duties to assure conditions under which populations will be as healthy as possible; it might reasonably be considered the body of law that creates a citizen's "right" to exist in a healthy environment. Falling within the realm of public health law are pollution control, reduction in violence, health education and disease prevention.

Gostin cites one recently published paper as an example of public health law. In the paper, he describes five models for legal government intervention intended to prevent injury and disease and promote the public's health. The *power to tax and spend* enables the government to set conditions for receiving and disbursing public resources. For example, federal highway funds are granted on the condition that states set the minimum drinking age at 21. With the *power to alter the informal environment,* the government can utilize labeling requirements to promote healthful consumer behavior. *Direct regulation of individuals* enforces regulations such as mandatory use of seat belts and motorcycle helmets, inspection of businesses and restaurants, and licensing of health-care professionals. *Use of the tort system on behalf of the public's health* becomes necessary when, for example, manufacturers, service providers and even government itself compromises the safety of consumer goods and services. Finally, through the process of *deregulation,* public health lawyers and legislators routinely examine and re-examine laws whose utility for the public health may be out-of-date or may have unnecessarily adverse consequences for business and the public's health.

A day in the life

There is enormous variety to Larry Gostin's workdays, although he can almost always count on putting in a sizable chunk of time researching and drafting major public health policy initiatives. "Presently, we're working on the Model Public Health Act, which concerns creating a public health preparedness and infrastructure for protecting the health and security of the nation in the event of a biological attack or a naturally occurring infectious disease of emergency proportions. Obviously, this work has become especially urgent since 9/11, and requires frequent conversations with people from the CDC as well as with governors, legislators at the federal, state and local levels, and other top decision makers," he says.

In addition to his policy formation activities and administrative duties, Gostin teaches weekly classes in human rights, constitutional law and public health law. He also serves on the advisory committees of several international and national agencies, such as the World Health Organization, the National Institutes of Health and the CDC.

In contrast to the broad, big-picture issues that occupy Gostin's attention, many public health lawyers deal predominantly with more day-to-day concerns. For example, someone in the office of general counsel at a state health department might begin her day with a meeting about a proposed nursing home closure because of sanitary code violations. Following the meeting, she and her staff might spend two hours reviewing licensing applications from out-of-state health care practitioners. Later in the morning, they may examine a complaint regarding illegal toxic waste disposal.

In the afternoon, she might drive to a hospital where she meets with the administrator to discuss granting a certificate of need to purchase an MRI machine because none exists within a two-mile radius.

Did you know? Law dealing with the power of government officials to take action to protect the public's health comes from four main sources: constitutions, statutes, regulations and judicial decisions. Each of these sources of law can be found at both the state and federal levels of government.[1]

"For any lawyer involved in public health, the rewards are really tremendous," says Gostin. "You know that your work is helping the public health infrastructure and playing a direct role in the betterment of people's lives. There is so much we in public health can do for people and populations. The law is the enabler of all that."

>>>> career at a glance

Lawrence O. Gostin, JD, LLD (Hon.)

2002–Present	**Visiting Scholar** Centre for Socio-Legal Studies, Oxford University
2000–Present	**Member** Institute of Medicine Panel, "Assuring the Health of the Public in the 21st Century"
2000–Present	**Director** Center for Law & the Public's Health at Johns Hopkins and Georgetown Universities (CDC Collaborating Center)
1996–Present	**Co-Director** The Johns Hopkins/Georgetown Program on Law and Public Health
1995–Present	**Professor of Law & Public Health** The Johns Hopkins University, School of Hygiene and Public Health
1993–Present	**Professor of Law** Georgetown University Law Center
1988–1994	**Associate Director** International Collaborating Center on Health Legislations, Harvard University/World Health Organization
1986–1994	**Executive Director** American Society of Law, Medicine & Ethics
1985–1994	**Adjunct Professor of Law and Public Health** Harvard University
1991–1993	**Vice Chair** Committee on the Use of Human Subjects in Research, Harvard School of Public Health
1989–1990	**Visiting Fellow** Centre for Socio-Legal Studies, Wolfson College, Oxford University
1987–1988	**Legislative Counsel** Labor and Human Resources Committee, Edward Kennedy, Chairman, United States Senate
1983–1985	**General Secretary** National Council for Civil Liberties (UK)
1982–1983	**Fellow in Psychiatry and Law** Centre for Criminological Research, Oxford University
1975–1982	**Legal Director** MIND (National Association for Mental Health) (UK)

1 http://www.jhsph.edu/bioterrorism/Bfaq_phlp.htm

public health
and the world

international and global health

It is said that we inhabit a shrinking planet. Technology has rendered borders and time zones irrelevant; most industries routinely operate in a global context. The number of people traveling abroad has reached more than 2 million a day.[1] People in New York, Paris, Nairobi and Tokyo eat much of the same fast foods, wear the same designer clothes, watch the same TV shows.

And one way or another, they are linked by many of the same health issues. In a world where virtually everything has become globalized, it is hardly

surprising that healthcare providers, research scientists and pharmaceutical companies have brought the eradication and treatment of disease into the global arena. Wherever they may work, whatever their chosen area of focus, every public health professional is part of an extraordinary global enterprise.

But exactly what is global health? The Washington, D.C.-based Institute of Medicine (IOM) defines it as "health problems and concerns that transcend national boundaries, may be influenced by circumstances or experiences in other countries, and are best addressed by cooperative actions and solutions."[2] The operative word is *transcend*: Global health is not the same as international health, which operates within and across borders and is always acutely conscious of them.

Rather, global health connotes a world where health problems and their solutions are increasingly borderless. To be sure, local political, economic and infrastructural realities must be acknowledged and dealt with, nation-by-nation. While environmentally related illnesses affect the whole world, there is no denying that they are more virulent and widespread in developing nations, where regulations are likely to be lax and sanitation facilities primitive. Nonetheless, Africa's AIDS epidemic, air pollution in Mexico City, childhood malnutrition in India, river blindness in Latin America, the specter of tainted beef in Europe all must be addressed as global problems, demanding globally coordinated efforts and the free exchange of information and ideas irrespective of borders.

Yet, whatever new ills it has inflicted upon the world, globalization made global health a far more pressing concern to political leaders. As recently as a decade ago, public health was rarely discussed at meetings of the G8 — the world's major industrialized nations. Today, says Dr. Nils Daulaire, president of the Global Health Council, "it is one of the fastest rising topics, and it's going to be one of the central issues in the future." Public health

organizations have begun to acknowledge the futility of decrying the rapid march of globalization, he says, and that it is more important "to learn how to harness its forces for the benefit of the needy."[3] At the same time, the world at large has begun to awaken to a reality that public health professionals have always recognized — that health is a prerequisite for economic growth, human dignity, the fulfillment of human rights, and world peace.

That isn't to suggest that health should overshadow all other concerns. But most of the world's luminaries, from rock stars and athletes to business leaders and heads of state, understand today that good health — and, more to the point, a global approach to public health — is essential for the secure future of the planet.

Clearly, global health is a work in progress. While substantial headway has been made against many of the most widespread and intractable health problems — communicable and infectious diseases like plague and influenza, substance abuse, environmental health, mental illness — they are still very much part of the global landscape.

The good news is that organizations and individuals working across political and geographic boundaries have scored some remarkable successes. For example, immunization programs have reduced and in some cases eliminated the presence of polio and other childhood diseases worldwide; by 1980, the World Health Organization (WHO) had succeeded in eradicating smallpox.[4] But as old problems are solved, new ones emerge and spread across borders, driven by behavioral or demographic changes, natural disasters, war and bioterrorism. Smallpox and other ancient diseases may have been banished, but in their place comes a new wave of universal scourges — HIV/AIDS, epidemic tuberculosis, food-borne diseases, and man-made environmental horrors such as acid rain and global warming. They affect the world in general, but reserve the bulk of their malevolence for developing nations. For example, malaria is on the increase in tropical countries because even one degree of global warming allows mosquitoes to breed in areas they could never have previously inhabited.

What is especially striking about today's global health picture are the ways in which human behavior is changing around the world, and the impact of those changes on people's health. At one end of the risk-factor scale lie conditions such as poverty, undernutrition, unsafe sex, unsafe water, poor sanitation and hygiene, iron deficiency and indoor smoke from solid fuels. These rank among the 10 leading causes of disease, and they are far more prevalent in the poorest countries and communities.

At the other end of the scale, one sees the price to pay for unhealthy consumption and the abuses of affluence. Excessive consumption of fat, sugar and salt lead to high blood pressure and high blood cholesterol, which are widely implicated in cardiovascular and cerebrovascular diseases. Smoking, obesity and excessive alcohol consumption heighten the danger. These factors are known all too well in the developed world; they are commonly viewed as middle and upper-income afflictions. The real drama is that they are becoming more prevalent in developing communities, where they lay a double burden on top of the infectious diseases that always have been the lot of poorer countries, according to Dr. Derek Yach, head of communicable diseases and mental health at the World Health Organization.[5] While tuberculosis today is the world's second most lethal infectious disease, claiming two million lives a year,[6] its impact has been surpassed by tobacco, which causes close to four million deaths a year.[7] That number will double by 2020, according to WHO projections, with 70 percent of smoking-related fatalities occurring in developing countries.[8]

Yet there is cause for optimism. The mapping of the human genome, completed in 2001, lays the groundwork for the development of new therapies for long-intractable diseases; the power of information technology is being harnessed more and more to deal with epidemics and other threats to global health. Disease persists, certainly, but there is no denying the world is a healthier place than it was a generation ago. Consider: During the past three decades, attention has focused on micronutritional issues — the roles of vitamins and minerals and how they can be delivered to nutrition-poor populations. Iodine deficiency in particular was a major cause of preventable mental retardation in millions of children in developing nations. But teams of scientists, health workers, policymakers and others working in close collaboration devised effective ways to introduce iodine into children's diets.

Admittedly, not all global health problems have responded so readily. The prevalence of AIDS, for example, has slowed many otherwise improving global health trends, such as infant, childhood and adult mortality rates. But the world is finally dealing with AIDS in an organized way, focusing on strategies that will provide access to short-term tools such as microbicides while it continues to fund research that will hopefully lead to cures or a vaccine.

Many international agencies and organizations are working to improve global health. Paramount among these is the World Health Organization, created in 1948 for the purpose of guaranteeing "the attainment by all people of the highest possible level of health." WHO's mission has translated into direct interventions and assistance whenever and wherever they are necessary, as evidenced most recently by its participation in fighting the outbreak of Ebola virus in Gabon in 2001. The United Nations Children's Fund (UNICEF), meanwhile, has done an outstanding job of focusing on the health problems of the world's children. In the early 1980s, UNICEF launched its "GOBI" initiative. "GOBI" stands for growth monitoring, oral rehydration, breastfeeding and immunizations; the agency boldly asserted that these four simple interventions could dramatically reduce the death toll of children worldwide. And they have been proven correct, time and again.

In a real sense, the terms "public health" and "global health" have become interchangeable. "In a world where nations and economies are increasingly interdependent, ill health in any population affects all peoples, rich and poor," notes the Institute of Medicine.[9] As WHO director-general Dr. Gro Harlem Brundtland elegantly reminds us, the rampant spread of infectious diseases such as AIDS, malaria and the West Nile virus give evidence that "in a globalized world, we all swim in a single microbial sea."[10]

Of course, public health has become globalized because disease has become globalized — and that fact underscores the necessity of working beyond the local level. That is, every community, large and small, can expect to be called upon to furnish resources and people to advance the global effort. In

a world of easy travel and vanishing trade restrictions, it is in the interests of developed countries to assist their developing neighbors. It isn't a simple matter of altruism or noblesse oblige but, rather, an understanding that the problems of one community threaten the whole world. "The world's nations, the United States included, now have too much in common to consider health as merely a national issue," notes the IOM.[11]

The simple fact is that global action against health risks in one country can help protect all people in all countries. That is the essence of global health in the 21st century.

Six billion people share a small and increasingly fragile planet, confronted by global health problems that may seem overwhelming. But they are all solvable problems. Global health professionals will be an integral part of the solution, whether working in a large urban hospital in Los Angeles, a rural clinic in the Midwest, or a field laboratory in Botswana.

The preceding essay is dedicated to global health pioneer William Foege, MD, MPH, who figured centrally in the effort to eradicate smallpox in the 1970s and later served as director of the U.S. Centers for Disease Control and Prevention.

An epidemiologist by training, Dr. Foege graduated from Pacific Lutheran University and subsequently earned an MD from the University of Washington Medical School in 1961 and an MPH from Harvard University in 1965. For the next decade, Dr. Foege's career carried him across the world in the fight against infectious diseases. After working in the campaign to eradicate smallpox in the 1970s, Dr. Foege became Chief of the CDC

Smallpox Eradication Program, and was appointed Director of the U.S. Centers for Disease Control and Prevention in 1977. Dr. Foege served as Director of the U.S. Centers for Disease Control and Prevention from 1977 to 1983.

In 1984, Dr. Foege and several colleagues formed the Task Force for Child Survival, a working group for the World Health Organization, UNICEF, The World Bank, the United Nations Development Program and the Rockefeller Foundation. Its success in accelerating childhood immunization led to an expansion of its mandate in 1991 to include addressing other issues that diminish the quality of life for children.

Dr. Foege was executive Director of the Carter Center from 1987 to 1992, where he remains a fellow and a senior health advisor. In January 1997, he joined the faculty of Emory University as Presidential Distinguished Professor of International Health at the Rollins School of Public Health. In September 1999, Dr. Foege became a Senior Medical Advisor for the Bill and Melinda Gates Foundation.

Dr. Foege holds honorary degrees from numerous institutions, and was named a fellow of the London School of Tropical Medicine and Hygiene in 1997. He is the author of more than 125 professional publications.

1 www.globalhealth.gov/quotes.shtml
2 www.globalhealth.gov/faq.shtml
3 http://www.who.int/bulletin/pdf/2001/issue9/new_features.pdf
4 http://www.who.int/emc/diseases/smallpox/factsheet.html
5 http://www.who.int/bulletin/pdf/2001/issue9/new_features.pdf
6 http://www.cdc.gov/nchstp/tb/worldtb2001/fact_sheet.htm
7 http://www.cdc.gov/od/oc/media/pressrel/r020412.htm
8 http://www.who.int/bulletin/pdf/2001/issue9/new_features.pdf
9 http://www.nap.edu/readingroom/books/avi/2.html
10 http://www.who.int/bulletin/pdf/2001/issue9/new_features.pdf
11 http://www.nap.edu/readingroom/books/avi/2.html

reproductive health specialist

A TRUE TALE

JoAnn Lewis, MPH, first learned about public health through the Peace Corps, which she joined directly after graduating from the University of

JoAnn Lewis, MPH

North Dakota. The Peace Corps put her through a rigorous crash course in health education techniques and language training in the U.S., the Virgin Islands and Trinidad. "It really was a life-changing experience," she says. After training with public health nurses in Trinidad, Lewis was sent to Niger, West Africa, where for two years she worked as a health educator, organized and ran prenatal and well-baby clinics and provided community health education. She spent a third year working as a health educator, and later as manager on a mobile

vaccination team, which was part of one of the last smallpox eradication programs in Africa. She completed her stint with the Peace Corps working to train new volunteers.

On her return to the U.S., she worked for the Department of Health, Education and Welfare's Office for Civil Rights for a year, before continuing her public health training at the Johns Hopkins School of Hygiene and Public Health, where she received her MPH in 1975. She then worked for Planned Parenthood of Metropolitan Washington, D.C. in its pregnancy

testing, counseling and referral service, and served as Coordinator for the Metropolitan Washington Family Planning Council. She came to Family Health International (FHI) in Research Triangle Park, North Carolina, 23 years ago, where she is currently Senior Vice President for Reproductive Health Programs.

"Some of the most important world issues facing family planning right now include emphasis on reproductive rights, and the need to assure that the use of family planning is voluntary."

Reproductive Health Specialist Checkpoint

Do the family- and macro-level issues of population control fascinate you?

Would you enjoy influencing human behavior in ways that benefit individuals and whole populations?

Does the idea of traveling to and working in developing countries appeal to you?

If so, read on

Profiling the job

A career in the field of reproductive health is most easily accessible through medical, educational or policymaking routes. Aspiring professionals might follow the medical route working in health care clinics, or community centers run by non-governmental organizations, community groups and government agencies. The educational path can include study at medical, pharmacy and nursing schools as well as in schools of public health. Governments and non-governmental organizations with global reach most often employ those interested in the policy aspects of the field.

Such organizations are the World Health Organization, the United Nations Population Fund and the International Planned Parenthood Federation.

The specific roles of reproductive health professionals depend on their particular areas of focus. A health educator might work to provide information and referral services, or possibly to provide health education at schools and to community organizations. In many countries, reproductive health specialists work in community programs rather than in clinics. They can be nurses, physicians, physician assistants or lay people trained to provide specific kinds of services. In fact, in many countries community-based distribution agents who are lay people provide the more basic methods of contraception — oral contraceptives, spermicides and condoms. "Typically, as long as providers are trained to offer basic information on how these methods work and what safety issues and potential side effects accompany them, much of this work can be done by supervised lay workers in places where local practice standards permit," says Lewis.

Students — particularly those in master's and doctoral programs — who are interested in working in global reproductive health, can apply for internships such as the Family Health International (FHI) internship program in special projects. Students can also gain experience through FHI's new program YouthNet, a global program committed to improving the reproductive health and HIV/AIDS prevention behaviors of youth 10-24 years of age.

Global reproductive health
The most broadly accepted definition of family planning is affording individuals and couples the means to have the number of children that they want. It is also a key strategy for reducing maternal mortality rates. Women

who have four or more pregnancies in their lifetime are much more likely to have severe health consequences or die in childbirth than women who have one or two children. In resource-deprived countries and in developed countries as well, there is a direct correlation between the number of children born to each mother and her children's chances of survival. Compared to children who have just one or two siblings, siblings whose birth dates are too close in time, and who are born into families where they must compete with many other children for resources, are much more likely to have poor survival rates.

According to Lewis, parents of smaller families find it easier to send all their children to school, gain employment outside of the home, earn enough income to provide some possibility of upward social mobility and in many instances just feed their children. "At a societal level, lower population growth maximizes the general resource base and the availability of services. Fewer children mean healthier children, less crowding in schools, less unemployment and less human impact on the environment," says Lewis.

Focusing on these and related issues, Family Health International works to improve reproductive and family health around the world through biomedical and social science research, innovative health service delivery interventions and training and information programs. The organization works in partnership with universities, ministries of health and non-governmental organizations to conduct ongoing projects in the U.S. and more than 40 developing countries.

According to Lewis, one of the most important world issues confronting family planning right now, and an issue of great importance at FHI, is the need to ensure that the use of family planning methods is voluntary. In the definition of family planning, emphasis must be placed on the words "number of children that the parents want," Lewis says, and adds, "this is not something that should be imposed by governments or external bodies." Two other issues of significant concern are contraceptive safety and assuring that people fully understand the choices they are making. "We try to ensure that people are given complete access to information concerning the various contraceptive and reproductive health choices that exist, how they work and what side effects they may have. These are quality of care issues, but they are also reproductive rights issues that people must understand fully so they will be able to make their own choices," she says.

Currently, Lewis' department at FHI is implementing a new, five-year worldwide program funded by USAID to improve reproductive health and prevent HIV infection among youth of 10 to 24 years of age. She has worked with the program staff to develop its technical strategies, set priorities for specific activities and plan for the resources needed to carry them out. Negotiation with various implementing partner agencies and frequent consultation with the donor agency are also included. In the near future, Lewis will travel to one of the countries requesting assistance through the program to identify which organizations there either are or could be involved, and to conduct needs assessments for youth reproductive health. She and her staff will meet with representatives of the host country government, various NGOs, and the local USAID representatives to achieve consensus on the plan and how it will be implemented.

A day in the life

As a Peace Corps volunteer in Africa and, later, through assignments with the federal government and Planned Parenthood of metropolitan Washington, JoAnn Lewis placed herself on what might be considered the front lines of public health. Today, as Senior Vice-President for Reproductive Health Programs at Family Health International, her responsibilities "are much more at a broad program level," she says.

Lewis oversees several divisions of FHI, including health services research, health behaviors research, information dissemination and training and the YouthNet program. She is also a main point of contact for financial donors, and figures centrally in resource development, strategic planning and partnering with other reproductive health agencies.

It's a big job and a critically important one, but Lewis doesn't do it alone. "I oversee — and am supported by — a large and tremendously talented professional staff located at our headquarters in North Carolina, a branch office outside Washington and several regional and county offices," she says. FHI's "extraordinarily varied and talented" workforce includes more than 500 physicians, clinicians, nurses, specialists in public health and adolescent health, social and behavioral scientists, anthropologists, demographers, economists, gender experts, epidemiologists, biostatisticians, trainers, instructional designers, journalists, social marketing experts and business professionals.

"Although we have personnel in the U.S. and abroad, most of our activities are international," Lewis says. "So I often need to address the concerns and program issues of our international offices." In particular, these can include assuring that field-based staff have the facilities and support they need to

carry out their work. "We also work hard at bridging cultural gaps between expatriate professionals and host-country governments and health ministries, so that a colloquial, two-way flow of health information is possible," she says.

On most days, Lewis will be called upon to advise FHI professionals on any number of matters, including protocols for conducting programs and behavioral research on issues related to reproductive health, family planning and contraceptive technology. Reviewing technical reports to donor agencies and making sure that funded programs "are on track and making progress toward their goals" are other important aspects of her job. She also reviews special reports and research papers before their submission for publication.

"The research arena that I oversee includes understanding reproductive risk behaviors and increasing the range and availability of contraceptive methods that are safe, effective, acceptable and affordable," Lewis says. "FHI also provides technical services and training programs for developing countries, especially in reproductive health and prevention and care services for people living with HIV/AIDS." Among her top priorities is assuring that research and programs are geared toward understanding the personal behaviors and motivations that cause people to use — or not use — particular methods or services.

It's hardly a surprise that Lewis is passionate about her work. "If you love to travel and expand your knowledge of other cultures — and I do — global public health is a wonderful field," she says. "And when the reports come in after a program has been implemented, and the numbers point to declines in unplanned pregnancies and maternal and infant mortality and morbidity, then you *know* you're in the right line of work."

"When people have smaller families, the resources available to the family have to be divided in fewer ways, so people can more easily send their children to school, women can be employed outside of the home and families have greater resources and perhaps access to some upward mobility at a societal level."

JoAnn Lewis, MPH

JoAnn Lewis, MPH

1991–Present	**Senior Vice President** Reproductive Health Programs Department, Family Health International, Research Triangle Park, N.C.
1987–1991	**Vice President of Programs** Family Health International
1984–1987	**Director of Field Development and Training** Family Health International
1983–1984	**Director of Field Support** Family Health International (formerly IFRP)
1980–1983	**International Projects Administrator** International Fertility Research Program
1978–1980	**Project Leader** Maternity Care Studies, International Fertility Research Program
1976–1977	**Research Analyst** JWK International Corporation
1974–1975	**Program Coordinator** Planned Parenthood of Metropolitan Washington
1972–1973	**Civil Rights Specialist** Health and Social Services, USDHEW Office of Civil Rights
1971–1972	**Co-director and Trainer** Peace Corps Public Health Training Program
1968–1971	**Volunteer Health Educator** Maternal and Child Health, U.S. Peace Corps

1 http://www.unfpa.org/mothers/contraceptive.htm
2 http://www.plannedparenthood.org/library/FAMILYPLANNINGISSUES/fpworldofdifference_fact.html

A TRUE TALE

For as far back as she can remember having considered her future career, Helene Gayle, MD, MPH, has been interested in society, policy and politics.

It was not until she attended medical school at the University of Pennsylvania that she was exposed to the field of public health. While attending her brother's graduation, Dr. Gayle was deeply struck by a speech delivered by Dr. D. A. Henderson, one of the leaders of the smallpox eradication campaign. "To hear someone like that, who was part of a team that has nearly eliminated an entire disease from the face of the earth, was incredible," she recalls. Dr. Henderson's words were a pivotal inspiration to Dr. Gayle's growing commitment to a career in public health.

Helene Gayle, MD, MPH

International HIV Specialist Checkpoint

Does working on one of the most complex and significant global health issues today appeal to you?

Are you interested in the sociology, economic and medical aspects of public health?

If so, read on

Dr. Gayle received her MPH from the Johns Hopkins University School of Hygiene and Public Health. She finished her pediatric residency at the Children's Hospital National Medical Center in Washington, D.C., and then went directly to the Epidemic Intelligence Service (EIS), part of the Centers for Disease Control and Prevention (CDC). Working in the EIS, she says, provides you with exceptional public health training. It also provided Dr. Gayle with a future. She continued at the CDC for the next 15 years, moving up the ranks through numerous positions. In addition to her time in the EIS, she completed a residency in preventive medicine, which included working in Africa on a program called Combating Childhood Communicable Disease. She then moved to the Pediatric and Family Studies Section of the CDC AIDS Program, doing research related to the investigation of HIV/AIDS in children, adolescents and women.

Among other positions Dr. Gayle held while at the CDC was Acting Special Assistant for Minority HIV Policy Coordination, in which she devised prevention strategies for U.S. racial and ethnic minority populations. The CDC also assigned her to the U.S. Agency for International Development (USAID) as the Director of their HIV/AIDS Division. She continued to work in HIV/AIDS-related pursuits, and in September 1995 became the Director of the National Center for HIV, STD and TB Prevention at the CDC.

Overseeing a staff of 1,400 including 500 field staff in national and international settings, Dr. Gayle provided scientific, managerial and policy leadership for surveillance, research, policies and interventions related to the prevention and control of these diseases. In September 2001, Dr. Gayle was detailed by the CDC to Seattle, Washington, where she is currently Director of the HIV/AIDS and TB Program at the Bill and Melinda Gates Foundation.

Aids in the global community

Two decades have passed since the first cases of HIV/AIDS were reported. Nothing paints a clearer picture of the fury of this still unpredictable epidemic than the global statistics. In 2000, there were 5.3 million new HIV infections worldwide and three million new deaths from the disease in that year alone.[1] In the same year, AIDS was the fourth leading cause of death in the world and the primary cause of death in Africa.[2]

Not all the news is bad, however. In countries that have mounted aggressive prevention campaigns, the rates of HIV infections have actually declined. Of the many current issues on the global front, one of the most pressing is how to effectively use what we know already works — and how to keep it going. "Sometimes," says Dr. Gayle, "even in countries where HIV rates are declining, there has not been a large enough infusion of resources nor a consistent enough political commitment to sustain the change. Keeping up with progress is critical and even more so when the tide begins to turn in our favor."

"Extraordinary opportunities are limitless for any public health professional who wants to get involved in the field of HIV/AIDS. Here one can truly make a difference."

Dr. Gayle believes it is urgent to continue promising AIDS-related research, such as vaccines and vaginal microbicide products, which women can use to protect themselves from infection. Care is another very crucial issue. "With at least 40 million people worldwide currently infected the need for care is going to be critical. We must devise better ways of providing care and support to people who are already HIV-infected, in addition to continuing to focus on stemming the wave of new infections."

In the United States, the future of the AIDS epidemic is uncertain. The number of AIDS cases and deaths, which were dropping with the use of efficacious pharmacotherapy, leveled off in 1998. We now have 793,026 AIDS cases in the United States since reporting began in 1981.[3] Case numbers may now be on the rise. "All the signs that we've been seeing for the last year or so suggest that there may in fact be resurgence in risk behavior leading to the potential for increase in HIV and AIDS in this country," says Dr. Gayle.

What is our greatest weapon in the war against AIDS? Dr. Gayle insists there is no one answer. Combating HIV and AIDS, she says, requires a comprehensive approach comprised of education, prevention, treatment, outreach and research.

"Clearly, government cannot go it alone," says Dr. Gayle. "One reason is that its resources will never be great enough. Another is that there are things that government, by definition, will have a harder time doing than private groups because private groups often have greater flexibility." Dr. Gayle is currently working at one such private entity, the Bill and Melinda Gates Foundation in Seattle, Washington. She is responsible there for research, policy and program issues on HIV, STDs and tuberculosis, the portfolio she had at the CDC. Part of her job is to determine the "comparative advantage" of the foundation. In other words, what should this organization be doing differently than other organizations? Where can it have the biggest impact? Dr. Gayle decides, from a grant-making perspective, who and which projects should be funded and how the Gates Foundation can form better coalitions with other foundations or with the public sector.

"There are things that government, by definition, will have a harder time doing than private groups because private groups often have greater flexibility."

Helene Gayle, MD, MPH

Limitless opportunities

According to Dr. Gayle, extraordinary opportunities abound for public health professionals who want to get involved in the field of HIV/AIDS, both domestically and globally. "Not only is this fascinating work, but here one can truly make a difference." People who are interested generally participate and specialize in one of three public health tracks: *research, programming* or *policy.* Research continues to be paramount in the fight against this disease, and there is always room in the field for people with a background in statistics, laboratory science, clinical care or epidemiology. Globally, a major focus of research is on vaccines, microbicides and drug development.

Did you know?
Today, 40
million people
are estimated
to be living
with HIV/AIDS.
Of these,
37.2 million
are adults,
17.6 million
are women,
and 2.7 million
are children
under 15.[4]

Public health students wishing to become involved in HIV/AIDS programs on a global scale can participate in a large number of arenas. Several years ago the CDC initiated a major HIV prevention and care program called the Global AIDS Program, which operates in over 20 countries in Africa, Asia and the Americas. Public health students can become involved in one of these CDC programs, or they can secure internships in ongoing research projects currently underway at different universities. Also, Dr. Gayle says, most schools of public health have programs that deliver services in the context of research and training in multiple countries throughout the world.

Public health professionals who prefer to work in the prevention arena might participate in different types of programs designed to treat and prevent the spread of HIV. These can include outreach programs to groups at high risk, media campaigns, education in school and the workplace, condom distribution, voluntary counseling and testing and partner notification.

Partner notification programs seek out sexual or needle-sharing partners of someone infected with HIV to inform them of their potential exposure and urge them to undergo testing, counseling and possibly treatment. Such programs identify at least some partners of most people seeking testing. The two main approaches of partner notification are patient referral, in which health officials counsel the individual on how to notify and refer partners to counseling, and testing and provider referral, in which health department personnel notify partners. In testing and provider referral, the health department preserves the anonymity of the source.

Numerous studies suggest that good counseling assists people to make informed decisions, cope better with their health conditions, and lead more positive lives, and prevents further transmission of HIV. Trained counselors sometimes provide HIV/AIDS counseling, though nurses and caregivers are often in the ideal position to offer effective advice and support.

An opportunity for counseling and treatment also exists with mother-to-child HIV transmission, the cause of the largest percentage of infections worldwide in infants and children, and thought to occur in pregnancy, during birth or through breastfeeding. Counselors advise HIV-infected women about the risks and benefits of breastfeeding to enable mothers to make informed decisions. Antiviral treatment, which reduces the transmission of HIV from a mother to her child, has been tremendously successful and is more likely to be the choice of women who receive effective counseling.

Additional opportunities exist to work in health and scientifically oriented governmental agencies and non-profit organizations, or international foundations. Some of the larger public sector settings include the CDC, the U.S.

Agency for International Development (USAID), the National Institutes of Health (NIH), the World Health Organization (WHO) and the World Bank, as well as the U.N. AIDS program — all of which are either technical resources or major funders. Major funders assist non-governmental organizations such as the Cooperative for Assistance and Relief Everywhere (CARE), Save the Children, AfriCare and national and grass roots organizations that are products of the countries themselves. For example, the CDC works with governmental and non-governmental agencies through its Global AIDS Program (GAP), which helps prevent HIV infection, improves care and provides necessary support to address the global HIV/AIDS pandemic in underdeveloped countries.

In the private sector, philanthropic agencies such as the Bill and Melinda Gates Foundation play important roles in the fight against HIV/AIDS and offer opportunities for involvement at every level. Employing "global grants," scholarships, and red tape-cutting coordination, the Gates Foundation promotes and accelerates promising medical research toward effective vaccines against HIV and other diseases and other technologies that primarily affect people in poor countries. Simultaneously, the Foundation contributes funding and supports efforts to facilitate greater availability and access to extant vaccines and treatments.

>>> career at a glance

Helene Gayle, MD, MPH

2001–Present	**Director** HIV/AIDS and TB, Bill and Melinda Gates Foundation, Seattle, WA
1995–2001	**Director** National Center for HIV, STD, and TB Prevention, Centers for Disease Control and Prevention
1995–1996	**Acting Director Division of HIV/AIDS Prevention** National Center for HIV, STD, and TB Prevention, Centers for Disease Control and Prevention
1994–1995	**Associate Director/Washington** Centers for Disease Control and Prevention
1992–1994	**Agency AIDS Coordinator and Chief** HIV/AIDS Division, United States Agency for International Development (USAID)
1990–1992	**Chief** International Activity Branch, Division of HIV/AIDS Prevention, National Center for HIV, STD, and TB Prevention, Centers for Disease Control and Prevention
1989–1990	**Assistant Chief for Science International Activity** Division of HIV/AIDS Prevention, National Center for HIV, STD, and TB Prevention, Centers for Disease Control and Prevention
1988–1989	**Acting Special Assistant for Minority HIV Policy Coordination** Office of the Deputy Director (HIV), Centers for Disease Control and Prevention
1987–1989	**Medical Epidemiologist** Pediatric and Family Studies Section, AIDS Program, Centers for Disease Control and Prevention
1986–1987	**Medical Epidemiologist** (Preventive Medicine Resident), Division of Evaluation and Research, International Health Program Office (IHPO), Centers for Disease Control and Prevention
1984–1986	**Epidemic Intelligence Service Officer** Epidemiology Branch, Division of Nutrition, Centers for Disease Control and Prevention

1 http://wwics.si.edu/NEWS/speeches/gayle.htm
2 http://wwics.si.edu/NEWS/speeches/gayle.htm
3 http://www.cdc.gov/hiv/stats.htm
4 www.cdc.gov/hiv/stats.htm

A TRUE TALE

James LeDuc, PhD, says he "blundered into public health" as a result of being in college during the Vietnam War, when the military was a prominent factor in young men's lives. Around the time he was graduating with a degree in zoology from California State University, Dr. LeDuc's mentor asked him if he wanted to work in West Africa for a few years on an army-sponsored contract under the jurisdiction of the Smithsonian Institution.

James LeDuc, PhD

During the next two years, he worked as a medical entomologist in the Ivory Coast and in Dahomey (now Benin). While in Africa, he received a direct commission into the military and for the next 23 years served as an officer in the Medical Service Corps of the U.S. Army Medical Research and Development Command. "Because I had both the opportunity to work closely with individuals and the opportunity to see the patterns of health problems throughout whole and different populations, those years in Africa inspired me to make public health my career within the service," Dr. LeDuc explains. "But I'm not unique, by any means. Many people I know ended up in public health because of similar experiences gained through their time in the Peace Corps."

Over the course of his career, Dr. LeDuc has worked as an epidemiologist and infectious disease specialist in some of the farthest reaches of the world, participating in many important public health initiatives that touch the lives and welfare of countless people. He did entomological and arbovirus research at the Walter Reed Army Institute of Research. In 1975, he began his PhD studies at UCLA. After receiving his doctorate in epidemiology in 1977, LeDuc commanded a Department of Defense medical research laboratory in Belem, Brazil, at the mouth of the Amazon River, and worked as chief of the arbovirus section in the virology department at the Gorgas Memorial Laboratory in Panama City, Panama. The programs he ran in Panama focused on diseases transmitted by arthropods, which involved field collections of mosquitoes, ticks and sand flies.

Tropical Disease Specialist Checkpoint

Are you looking for adventure coupled with challenge?

Do you like to travel?

Are you willing to work in situations that are sometimes difficult?

Does the prospect of working closely with people from different cultures intrigue you?

If so, read on

LeDuc retired from the Army in 1992 and began working for the Centers for Disease Control and Prevention (CDC) as an epidemiologist, and was detailed by the CDC to the World Health Organization (WHO) in Geneva, Switzerland. As a medical officer, he worked on emerging infectious diseases that continue to pose problems in many parts of the world. He moved to the CDC in Atlanta in 1996 as Associate Director for Global Health within the National Center for Infectious Diseases (NCID), and in 2000, became Director of the Division of Viral and Rickettsial Disease at the NCID, his current position.

During the course of his career, Dr. LeDuc has participated in many public health initiatives. For example, he played a role in establishing programs at the CDC, the Pan American Health Organization and the World Health Organization (WHO) on emerging infectious diseases, worked with the World Bank to improve disease surveillance in developing countries and tracked Ebola virus in Africa. He is also a highly regarded specialist on viral hemorrhagic fevers and has devoted much of his time recently to the process of ensuring that the United States will have sufficient smallpox vaccine, should the need ever arise for large quantities.

"To do well in global health, you must have knowledge of the cultural as well as the scientific aspects of disease prevention and health care delivery, particularly in developing parts of the world."

Profiling the job

Before setting foot in the tropics or elsewhere abroad, the successful global health professional should acquire a set of core skills that includes a background in epidemiology (especially epidemiology of infectious diseases), nutrition, biology, public health communications/education and ecology, according to Dr. LeDuc. It is essential to understand the specific challenges posed by the more prevalent global diseases such as malaria, tuberculosis and, particularly, AIDS. Knowledge of the cultural and scientific aspects of disease prevention and health care delivery is essential, especially in developing parts of the world. Finally, basic understanding of economics and accounting is always useful, especially for those professionals who will manage large budgets and/or grants.

Global health is an exciting option for individuals who thrive on adventure and challenge. Physicians, pharmacists and nurses are always needed, but so are epidemiologists, sanitarians and program managers. Biologists and ecologists are necessary because they understand the health impact that may result from such events as dam construction and reservoir excavations.

Likewise, medical entomologists who understand how mosquitoes and other insects transport and transmit diseases, and parasitologists who are experts in how parasites cause disease, are also essential.

Global public health offers unparalleled opportunities for travel. Practitioners can find work in the tropics or in northern climates, in the jungles of Africa or on the streets of Bangladesh. Work is available in governmental agencies such as the CDC, USAID, the military services or non-governmental agencies. Such agencies include the Carter Foundation, whose health work is accomplished through its International Task Force for Disease Eradication; the Bill and Melinda Gates Foundation, a grant-making foundation that supports initiatives in education, world health and population, and community; Cooperation for Assistance and Relief Everywhere (CARE), which, among its many missions, delivers emergency medical relief; and WHO, which stimulates and advances work on the prevention and control of epidemic, endemic and other diseases.

The field is also exceptional for its occasional exotic travel opportunities and its professional challenges, says Dr. LeDuc. "One day you're doing seroepidemiology of hantaviruses and population dynamics of mammal communities in Baltimore, and the next day, you're consulting on the same type of virus in a severely ill patient in Greece." Dr. LeDuc describes a recent incident in which a man from Texas died of yellow fever after returning home from an Amazon River fishing trip. Health authorities were concerned that this episode might launch an outbreak in the United States. Physicians, pathologists and epidemiologists from the Texas State Department of Health sprang into action. Blood and tissue specimens were sent to the CDC for laboratory evaluation. Once yellow fever was verified, the Pan American Health Organization and Brazil's public health officials were immediately contacted,

Did you know?
The Hospital for Tropical Diseases dates its origins to the old British Royal Navy warship HMS Grampus, which in 1821 was turned into a floating hospital for the treatment of tropical and infectious diseases.[1]

and conference calls were set up between the Texas state epidemiologist, the state laboratory and CDC experts. "For us," says Dr. LeDuc, "the vital next step was to track this man's activities from the day he departed the Amazon to the day he died in Texas."

Since mosquitoes transmit yellow fever, the man's hometown was placed on mosquito control alert. The travel industry was brought in to identify everyone else on the man's fishing tour and these people were contacted. This case is a good lesson in tropical medicine, says Dr. LeDuc. For someone considering a career in global public health, it is an excellent example of how many different people and occupations are integrated in a large-scale cross-border epidemiological investigation, and how much each relies on the other.

Tracking Ebola virus

In 1995, Dr. LeDuc was working in Geneva for WHO when he received a telephone call from the communicable disease chief of service at the WHO office in Brazzaville, Republic of the Congo. The chief described people dying in large numbers from what appeared to be a sudden outbreak of a type of hemorrhagic fever.

What happened, Dr. LeDuc explains, was that a medical laboratory technician working in a clinical laboratory at a hospital in Kikwit, Zaire, became infected from a blood specimen drawn from a patient whose disease's etiology no one could explain. The lab technician had fallen suddenly ill. Because he was a hospital staff member, many of his co-workers wanted to be involved in his care, and when he became sicker, physicians performed exploratory surgery. This proved a tragic mistake, because all of the operating room personnel became infected, too. When these people in turn became ill, those caring for them were also exposed to the virus. The number of deaths escalated rapidly.

When Dr.LeDuc was notified at WHO in Geneva, he suspected the cause to be the Ebola virus and immediately called the CDC in Atlanta, considered throughout the world to be the gold standard in handling such outbreaks. The WHO and CDC together sprang into action, sending a full response team to the African site. Because there is no vaccine for Ebola, it was essential to interrupt its transmission, which meant isolating infected patients and protecting any new incoming health care workers with barrier clothing and equipment. "We needed gloves, gowns and money to hire local help so they could go out and actually do the case finding. After obtaining the necessary equipment and supplies, our first tasks were to set up systems for managing the virus within the hospital and lab. Then we went out into the community to locate new cases," says Dr. LeDuc. This meant stopping at every house to determine if there were sick people inside, moving them to an isolation ward and then following the "chains of transmission" — finding every single person who had come in contact with each patient and the people whom *they* had contacted. In the meantime, Dr. LeDuc was busy dealing with the world press coverage of the outbreak while keeping eager reporters away to avoid transmission from the Ebola patients.

A crucial part of his challenge was to trace where the outbreak had started. A team of ecologists and biologists was sent into the forest where the first patient — the "index case" — had been working. They collected "everything that moved and much that did not," LeDuc says. Though epidemiologists and microbiologists tested thousands of collected specimens, none proved positive for Ebola, so the source was never found. Fortunately, the outbreak was contained through the heroic efforts of local physicians and nurses working in concert with the medical and public health professionals from WHO Geneva and Brazzaville and the CDC. At the end of the 1996 outbreak some 250 lives had been lost.[2] This outbreak would probably have been a far greater disaster had not an organized global health community intervened. While most careers in tropical medicine and public health may not be involved in such a dramatic scenario, many professionals in this field enjoy interesting, exciting and professionally rewarding careers.

A day in the life
As Director of the Division of Viral and Rickettsial Diseases, Dr. LeDuc's day includes many administrative responsibilities which, to the casual observer, might seem tedious but are, according to Dr. LeDuc, engaging and fascinating — there's never a dull moment for a division director. Just as when Dr. LeDuc worked for WHO and faced an Ebola outbreak with equanimity and professionalism, today he similarly represents his division with other colleagues in the CDC, to other government agencies, and to the global health community concerning health issues and infectious disease outbreaks worldwide. Dr. LeDuc lectures, consults, and shares his expertise in infectious disease and public health at meetings and symposia across the globe. Recently, he has devoted much of his time to assuring the public of the CDC's preparedness in the aftermath of the events of September 11, 2001.

Did you know?
An estimated fourteen million people die from treatable infectious and parasitic diseases every year, a quarter of all deaths worldwide. Over 90% of the victims live in developing countries.[3]

He recently gave testimony before the Senate Appropriations Committee regarding bioterrorism preparedness and what the CDC's public health response would be to terrorist use of smallpox.

As director of his division, Dr. LeDuc oversees a staff of about 500 people, some of whom spend much of their time in the field, as Dr. LeDuc did in his earlier days. He describes one staff member's involvement with the Hong Kong flu virus several years ago, upon the outbreak of a brand-new strain. Transmitted from chickens, the virus had been identified as the source of infections and deaths of otherwise healthy Hong Kong citizens. The epidemiologist flew to Hong Kong and was named project manager to work jointly with his counterparts in the Hong Kong Ministry of Health. The only way to stem the epidemic, local experts and the CDC decided, was to depopulate all markets in Hong Kong of chickens, close the markets and sterilize the city's chicken pens. Dr. LeDuc says the strategy worked; no more human cases were seen. Many public health professionals, particularly those in the field of influenza, felt that quick action saved the world from an influenza pandemic. "That is the kind of work that a global health specialist does," Dr. LeDuc says, "saving not just single lives but populations of lives. It's really a remarkable opportunity."

>>> >> ## career at a glance

James LeDuc, PhD

2000–Present	**Director** Division of Viral and Rickettsial Diseases, National Center for Infectious Diseases, the Centers for Disease Control and Prevention
1996–2000	**Associate Director for Global Health** National Center for Infectious Diseases, the Centers for Disease Control and Prevention
1992–1996	**Medical Officer** Communicable Diseases Division, World Health Organization, Geneva, Switzerland
1981–1992	**Director** Disease Assessment Division, U.S. Army Medical Research Institute of Infectious Diseases, Fort Dietrick, Maryland, and other related positions

1 http://thehtd.org
2 http://www.msnbc.com/news/686255.asp?cp1=1#BODY
3 www.neglecteddiseases.org/thecrisis.shtml

limitless
opportunities

the importance of partnership
in the public health system

The public health system is like a complex multidimensional puzzle — all the pieces must fit together to make a sensible whole. To achieve successful outcomes, professionals and organizations in the public and private sectors, the interlocking components of the puzzle, must work together. While cooperation among the sectors has always been a cornerstone to advancing the health of the public as the world and health issues become more complex and resources scarcer, the need for creative strategic partnerships in all aspects of public health has never been greater.

By Bobbie
Berkowitz,
PhD, RN, FAAN,
Professor
and Chair,
Department of
Psychosocial
and Community
Health,
University of
Washington
School of
Nursing,
Director,
Turning Point
National
Program Office,
Robert Wood
Johnson
Foundation

Bobbie Berkowitz, PhD, RN, FAAN

The health of a nation's citizens has long depended on the willingness of professionals in disparate fields to share information. Bringing together professionals whose particular focus has given them different ways of thinking, methods and strategies builds a smarter and more knowledgeable health care constituency. Since the range of factors that influences people's health can seldom be addressed adequately by only one organization or program, a multidisciplinary approach to providing public health services has grown in importance. Collaboration and cooperation are also imperative in an era when funding is tight even in developed countries, and when all jurisdictions are being asked to do more with the resources available. The main goal of public health partnerships, therefore, is to creatively bring together organizations, agencies, people and themes to implement strategies for change to improve the health of our people, and to strengthen our prevention abilities.

Partnering among public health professionals yields many benefits including advances in disease prevention, and a stronger public health infrastructure.

Disease prevention

To prevent disease, we professionals must base our judgments on good data. We must use scientific studies supported by methodical and meticulous data collection and evaluation. Currently, we are all too often relegated to the use of data collected in institutional isolation, using multiple methods and multiple standards for which each institution has its own set of variables.

Hospitals, health departments and academic institutions can collect data simultaneously, but without a cooperative, uniform system these data cannot be used to form valid conclusions. Much laboriously collected data is wasted because the research is based on different standards, and so the opportunity to examine a larger, more significant population is missed. Bringing together scientists and researchers in a partnership would allow them to set uniform standards for data collection.

A strong public health infrastructure

Public health infrastructure is composed primarily of information systems, the public health workforce, and organizational structures. These components work together to form the base of our public health system. We have many examples of how partnerships can improve the functioning of the public health infrastructure. Informations system capacity is particularly important. Providers within the system need to collaborate rapidly around the collection, analysis, and reporting of data related to communicable disease control. Suppose, for example, a community physician sees a patient with a high fever and symptoms suggesting encephalitis. The physician would then send a blood sample to a laboratorian. Once the specimen is identified, the laboratory professional would quickly report that information not only back to the physician, but also to the appropriate public health agencies, on the theory that there might be an impending outbreak. This day-to-day practice, taken in the context of a cooperative public health environment can — and often does — result in saving many lives in communities throughout the country. In fact, Illinois recently experienced such an event. Several private laboratories began reporting an outbreak of salmonella. Astute contact between public health professionals at the Centers for Disease Control and Prevention in Atlanta and public health personnel in neighboring midwestern states revealed that the source of contamination was commercially prepared toasted oat cereal. The simultaneous gathering of information in Illinois and a number of other states led to a speedy identification of this public health threat. Further, this threat was followed by close collaboration with businesses to coordinate a broad recall of the product.[1] Clearly the day-to-day collaboration between private practice professionals, private industry and government public health personnel saved the lives of many citizens.

A skilled workforce is another essential component of the public health infrastructure. Public health professionals are scattered throughout the country, working in agencies, institutions, businesses and the field at the local, state and national levels. This wonderful diversity of public health

expertise provides our country with a rich network of knowledge, skills, talent and perspective. It is imperative for all levels to work together to define the skills and competencies expected from our public health workforce so the public can be assured, at least in part, that the members of this workforce, no matter where they are, exhibit the highest level of proficiency. One of the innovative ways that this might be accomplished is through uniform

credentialing, which Dr. Kristine Gebbie addresses in the next chapter. The need for other innovative approaches to focus the energy and skills of our diverse public health resources will be a key strategy to advancing the public health agenda in this country, and an enabling strategy for reaching out to others less advantaged in needy regions of the world.

Organizational structures must be designed to improve the efficiency and quality of the system. This requires partnering not only among professionals, but also among various organizations and agencies. For example, a concerned community, a local hospital, a state health department and the federal government might cooperate to create a new public health clinic. For years, uninsured citizens without access to care for even the most basic medical needs have used the hospital emergency room in place of a primary care physician. A state public health department can alleviate such costly overutilization by partnering with that hospital — and perhaps even the local chamber of commerce or private industry — to secure a federal grant that would enable the development of a low-income clinic under the hospital's administrative auspices. Such a setup would provide access to quality medical care for those in need, while fulfilling the mission of the hospital and the local public health department. It would also serve private sector partners well by helping them keep their workforce productive while utilizing health benefit programs more cost effectively.

The Turning Point Initiative, a program I direct, is an example of a national effort to strengthen and improve the public health infrastructure so it is able to focus on health promotion, disease prevention, and the protection of the public from threats and hazards to health. The program, funded by The Robert Wood Johnson Foundation, is a national public health initiative comprising 23 states, and promises to have a potent impact on the future of public health care. This important initiative addresses the need to improve effective interaction among many components of the public health system. Collaborative models bring together these partners to plan and develop strategies for system change. Through this program, we expect a transformation and strengthening of the public health infrastructure so that states, local communities and their public health agencies can be more responsive to health threats and challenges. The goal of Turning Point is ambitious, but crucial. Such a strategically driven process will form one possible model for other states and communities to use. Restructuring public health outreach in a strategic and cost-efficient manner must be done in a way that addresses emerging public health needs and corrects longstanding health deficiencies.

The effectiveness of our future public health system depends largely on the ability of organizations and professionals to form strong collaborative relationships, both public and private. Today more than ever, through initiatives such as Turning Point and the willingness of entities within the system to work together, we are in an ideal position to see the formation of distinct and useful partnerships. I can only hope that these unions will continue to grow and flourish throughout the next ten years.

Bobbie Berkowitz, PhD, RN, FAAN is professor and chair of the Department of Psychosocial and Community Health at the University of Washington School of Nursing. Dr. Berkowitz is currently Director of the Robert Wood Johnson Foundation's Turning Point National Program Office.

Dr. Berkowitz was Deputy Secretary of the Washington State Department of Health from 1993 to 1996, and was Chief of Nursing Services for the Seattle-King County Department of Public Health from 1986 to 1993. She has served on the Washington State Board of Health, the Washington Health Care Commission, the American Nurses' Association Committee on Community-Based Indicators, and as co-Chair of the Institute of Medicine's National Committee on Monitoring and Improving the Health of Communities. She currently serves on the boards of the Hanford Environmental Health Foundation, Qualis Health, and the Public Health Foundation.

Dr. Berkowitz is a fellow in the American Academy of Nursing, a member of the Institute of Medicine and served on the Cabinet on Nursing Administration of the Washington State Nurses Association, and on the Governing Council of the Public Health Nursing Section for the American Public Health Association.

Berkowitz holds bachelor's and master's degrees in nursing from the University of Washington and a PhD in nursing from Case Western Reserve University in Ohio.

1 http://www.idph.state.il.us/public/press98/salm.htm

academic nurse leader

**Academic
Nurse Leader
Checkpoint**

Are you
dedicated to
nursing?

Do you prefer
to apply your
nursing skills to
broader popu-
lations rather
than individual
patients?

Do you
welcome the
challenge of
training others
to follow in
your footsteps,
contributing to
the health of
populations?

Does interact-
ing with people
from a wide
array of other
disciplines
excite you?

If so, read on

A TRUE TALE

When she was three, Kristine Gebbie, DrPH, RN, told her family she
was going to be a nurse, and she never wavered from that conviction. She
attended St. Olaf College's nursing program
in Northfield, Minnesota, which she felt gave
her a broad preparation for her profession.

At the University of California in Los
Angeles, Dr. Gebbie added a master's degree
in community mental health to her credentials. For several years, she worked and
taught nursing hospital management in Los
Angeles and St. Louis, but soon found that
she was so committed to disease prevention
that hospital work, though deeply rewarding
for some health professionals, just wasn't for
her. "Personally, the challenges of impacting
individual health through contributing to the

Kristine M. Gebbie, DrPH, RN

health of populations seemed more tantalizing than the day-to-day hospital
responsibilities I was dealing with." says Dr. Gebbie. In 1978, an advertise-
ment for a position commissioned by the state of Oregon to run the state
public health system caught her eye. She applied, and three months later
became the director of public health for the State of Oregon.

Dr. Gebbie spent 11 years in Oregon. In 1989, she went to Washington
State for four years to help set up a new state public health department, and
then to Washington, D.C., where she was the first Director of the National
AIDS Policy Office of the White House and Senior Consultant on Public
Health Initiatives to the Office of Public Health and Science.

Dr. Gebbie arrived in New York City in 1995 to be an Associate Professor
of Nursing at the Center for Health Policy at the Columbia University
School of Nursing, a position she currently holds.

A colleague once asked Dr. Gebbie why she left nursing to go into public
health. "Actually, I never left nursing," she answered, explaining that she
brought her nursing background to public health practice. "I think that's an
important message for all health professionals. When you choose public

health, you do not quit being a nutritionist, or a social worker, or a pharmacist, or a physician or a nurse. Your commitment to caring for people is still paramount — you simply are applying it to broader populations instead of individual patients."

Professionals in public health

Today, nearly any health-related discipline interacts with the field of public health in one way or another. Nurses comprise one of the largest single groups of professionals practicing public health. Others include environmentalists and physicians, social workers, nutritionists, pharmacists, dentists, laboratory specialists, epidemiologists and biostatisticians. There are vast differences in the training and expertise of public health professionals, differences determined not just by their specialties, but also by the settings in which they choose to practice.

Dr. Gebbie suggests the easiest and optimal way for professionals to successfully transition from clinical practice into public health is to obtain supplementary training. There is a movement afoot — known as "uniform credentialing" — to provide comprehensive, basic public health education to all health professionals, without requiring them to return to school for a master's in public health (MPH). Professionals also can enhance their skills in public health through distance-learning formats, web-based learning, continuing education courses and on the job.

As opposed to one-on-one clinical practice, public health practitioners are trained to look not so much at individuals, but at populations with shared health care needs. By treating the populations, they treat the individuals en masse. When treating individuals directly, public health practitioners look at how they fit into a population's health-need profile. "If a nurse has been classically trained in working with mothers and babies in a hospital clinic, and then chooses, without public health training, to work in a community child health program, she may have some difficulty understanding and appreciating the concepts of birth

"When you choose public health, you do not quit being a nutritionist, or a social worker, or a pharmacist, or a physician or a nurse. Your commitment to caring for people is still paramount — you simply are applying it to broad populations instead of individual patients."

rates and high risk or vulnerable populations," Dr. Gebbie says. Still, there are many vacancies for public health nurses, and often the only specific educational requirement for a position is a degree in nursing, preferably the Bachelor of Science (BSN). Holders of two-year associate nursing degrees (ADNs) should add the additional two years needed for a full four-year degree if they want to enter public health nursing, according to Dr. Gebbie. "But then the ADN holder has the advantage of taking courses in public health in those two later years."

As new schools of public health open, even experienced public health professionals are considering additional training to either extend their existing knowledge or to learn new skills. Dr. Gebbie cites three competencies that have recently emerged in response to perceived voids in the public health system: informatics, law and genetics. The field of public health informatics has grown rapidly to keep up with advances in information technology. Public health relies increasingly on sophisticated computer systems, which provide such tools as automatic reporting of notifiable conditions and dissemination of data from and among health surveillance investigations. There is currently a need for accelerated development of systems that facilitate communication among public health personnel at all levels, so that data can be used appropriately and efficiently.

Professional needs in the public health arena are not confined to the field of medicine, therapeutics and sociology. Public health law is another burgeoning field. "The laws and regulations that govern public health also need to be looked at carefully," Dr. Gebbie says. "In many cases, regulations and statues are woefully out-of-date, and review is essential." A large and diverse array of laws and government policies affect public health directly and indirectly, such as those that regulate food safety, clean water, land use and childhood immunizations. Training to provide new competencies in public health law is being developed for attorneys who are part of the public health workforce, or who act as independent consultants for health departments.

Know any molecular biologists? Dr. Gebbie points out that there are public health career options for these professionals as well. Genetics and genomics have entered the public health spotlight as a result of the completion of the first phases of the human genome project (HGP). Public health professionals wonder how and to what extent this genetic knowledge can improve their ability to practice prevention in the community. For example, how do genetic determinants contribute to the occurrence of a particular disease category or endpoint? Do given diseases cluster in families or in a certain community? How do we obtain and utilize individual genetic information without compromising basic rights to privacy? Detailed knowledge of gene structures may lead to answers to many such questions, and public health practitioners are now identifying ways to take advantage of geneticists' work.

As the field of public health expands, another issue under discussion in public health circles is how to identify competencies for a specific job. Dr. Gebbie calls *credentialing* "the primary way to identify practitioners who

are truly competent in a given area." She adds, "This is not to say a practitioner can't be perfectly good at epidemiology without having an epidemiology degree. But such a degree makes it so much easier to be confident in that person's competency." A new type of credentialing is currently under discussion. "This credentialing would certify that a professional understands what population-based practice means, knows at least minimally how to use epidemiology and other data to understand a community's health status, and knows about effecting prevention on a broad scale," says Dr. Gebbie. At present, no procedure or certification process satisfies verification of these requirements other than the MPH degree itself.

"Uniform credentialing," as the process is known, still remains a concept. Progress made thus far has taken a great deal of collaboration among federal agencies such as the Centers for Disease Control and Prevention (CDC) and professional organizations such as the American Public Health Association (APHA), Association of State and Territorial Health Officials (ASTHO) and various schools of public health, to determine the best way to credential public health personnel. Still, questions remain. What kind of examination should be required? What kind of work experience is sufficient? Who actually determines whether a certificate should be issued? These organizations have

successfully identified and codified a list of core public health competencies, a clear benefit to any public health employer seeking a method to identify qualified workers. Some of the competencies and skills deemed necessary for the effective delivery of essential public health services are:

- *Analytic/Assessment* — defines a problem and uses data to determine an effective solution

- *Policy Development/Program Planning* — develops and translates policy into plans and programs

- *Communication* — communicates effectively, both in writing and orally, and grasps how the media communicates information

- *Cultural Competency* — is sensitive to persons from diverse cultural, racial and socioeconomic backgrounds as well as persons of all ages and lifestyle preferences

- *Community Dimensions of Practice* — identifies how public and private organizations operate within a community

- *Basic Public Health Sciences* — understands the health status of populations and factors contributing to health promotion and disease prevention

- *Financial Planning and Management* — uses human relations skills for management and motivation of personnel, and knows how to develop and present a budget

- *Leadership and Systems Thinking* — creates a culture of ethical standards within organizations and communities, promotes team and organizational learning and contributes to development, implementation and monitoring of organizational performance standards

Teamwork

With so many diverse professions and backgrounds contributing to the public health landscape, it's no wonder that effective teamwork is one of the hallmarks of public health excellence. And for Dr. Gebbie, the dynamic interdisciplinary nature of the field is one of its most stimulating attributes. Over the near term, the increasing number of diverse professionals who play many roles within the system will likely add greater dimension and effectiveness to the public health field.

"Ideally, there should be a fluid back and forth movement of practitioners across functions, so that a visitor can walk into a medium-sized health department, watch the multidisciplinary staff going about their daily business and, with a few exceptions, find it difficult to determine who is in what profession," says Dr. Gebbie. "The person running the epidemiology program may have been originally trained as a veterinarian. The department head for the family planning outreach program may have originally been trained as a pharmacist. The organizer of the epidemiological investigation of a food-borne outbreak may have originally been trained as a nurse."

Working together as a team is the key to getting things done. "Not all of us learned terribly well from our basic education how to work together. We tended to be so busy just learning our specialties that we didn't pay much attention to what other people were doing. When you get into public health practice, you really do have to learn how to interact with people from all other disciplines, respect what they bring to the table, be proud of what you bring, and know how to put all the pieces together in new and different ways." Dr. Gebbie uses her friends who were trained in medicine and pharmacy as an example of such teamwork. "When we sit together, tossing around ideas about what we would like to do to perfect the world of public health, you might not guess who does what from listening to what each of us says, just because we've become so much more knowledgeable about our respective fields. But, if you listen very closely, you start hearing both distinct professional perspectives and how we are able to pull those perspectives together to make a whole that we think works exceptionally well. Or as the old saying goes, 'the whole is more than the sum of its parts.'"

A day in the life

New research models, bioterrorism, team-building skills, food-borne disease — all of these and many more can play a role in a "typical" day on the job for Dr. Gebbie. "I suppose you might say my day, in varying increments, is one of practice, education and research," says Dr. Gebbie. "It's truly a mixture of responsibilities, the proportions of which depend on whether it is primarily a teaching day or a research day." A teaching day may find Dr. Gebbie preparing a lecture or instructing doctoral students how to think in new ways about research. Likewise, a research day involves meeting with the team to plan for various projects, "involving esteemed experts from across the country."

The day of a public health nurse working in the field would be vastly different. She would probably spend at least part of the day in a public health clinic, providing immunizations, examining children or diagnosing sexually transmitted diseases. She might spend part of her day seeing patients in non-clinic settings — a community center, a church basement, a shopping center or even a person's home. A public health nurse, during a typical week, participates in at least one group education event, such as an HIV prevention lecture at a high school, a prenatal class at the community center or a blood pressure screening at a senior citizen's meeting place. There is enormous demand for public health nurses to go out into the community as speakers, Dr. Gebbie says. "These days, there are simply not enough nurses to go around."

>>> ## career at a glance

Kristine M. Gebbie, DrPH, RN

1997–Present	**Associate Professor, Director of Doctoral Studies & Director** Center for Health Policy, Columbia University School of Nursing
1994–1999	**Senior Advisor** Public Health Functions, Office of Public Health and Science, U.S. Department of Health and Human Services
1993–1994	**National AIDS Policy Coordinator** The White House
1989–1993	**Secretary of Health** State of Washington
1978–1989	**Administrator** Health Division, Oregon Department of Human Resources (equivalent to state health commissioner)
1976–1978	**Assistant Director** St. Louis University Hospitals
1972–1977	**Assistant Professor** St. Louis University School of Nursing
1974–1976	**Director** Ambulatory Care, St. Louis University Hospitals
1968–1971	**Instructor/Lecturer** UCLA School of Nursing

PUBLIC HEALTH TRAINING

Is a degree in public health necessary to practice public health? Many of the professionals profiled in this book have gained their skills through on the job training and not necessarily through master's or doctoral degree programs. These professionals are making a significant difference in the public's health in the U.S. and throughout the world. It should be noted, however, that further and higher education continue to be of high importance to bettering a lifetime of experiential learning. It is true that some capabilities can only be inculcated through experience, but it is equally true that other strengths and abilities require formal instruction. As your career advances and you become fascinated with new subject matter encountered in your work, it is likely — but again, not absolutely required — that you will seek masters, doctorates and certifications requiring additional training.

Barbara
DeBuono,
MD, MPH,
Senior Medical
Director/
Group Leader,
Public Health,
Pfizer Inc.

practicing public health in the private sector

Future advances in public health will come not only from new clinical research but, increasingly, from the creation and application of population-based prevention programs, initiatives and partnerships. While many of these are the work of public health organizations and associations, the private sector is making a significant contribution. It is to this area that my personal journey in public health has led, and I find it dynamic, challenging and rewarding.

Barbara A. DeBuono, MD, MPH

The pharmaceutical industry, and Pfizer in particular, are responsible for some very noteworthy private sector programs and partnerships currently underway. While Pfizer is best known to health professionals for discovering, developing and manufacturing pharmaceuticals for use by individual patients, the company is also committed to improving the health of populations. Because a population is more than the sum of its individuals, that commitment is accomplished by addressing community as well as patient issues.

Through the implementation of programs created by public health professionals within Pfizer, and through our relationships with thought leaders, public agencies and community organizations, we work to leverage our company's assets to improve the public's health. Since I benefit from dual perspectives — having worked in both the public and private sectors — I can see firsthand how important and effective these initiatives are.

Before coming to Pfizer, I worked for many years in government, having served as Director of the Rhode Island Department of Health and as Commissioner of Health for the State of New York under Governor George Pataki. I also held an executive position at New York-Presbyterian Healthcare Network and an appointment as a professor of medicine. The reason I decided four years ago to go into the private sector is perhaps no different than that which led many people down the same path: it provided me with a new opportunity to work on solving some of the most important issues connected to health care from a whole different angle. The bonus is that I am able to do this with a successful company's commitment and resources behind me.

As senior medical director of public health, I serve the company both externally and internally. Among the most important external aspects of my job is to build relationships with public health thought leaders and to create and manage non-product-related programs for the public health community. For example, I have led a comprehensive Pfizer initiative in health literacy, a vital component for successful health care delivery. The Pfizer Health Literacy Initiative (PHLI) operates to ensure that patients have a clear understanding of their illness so they may make effective health care choices. A health-literate patient understands how to manage his or her illness, how to follow directions about diet and medication compliance, how to read a consent form and how to effectively communicate with physicians. Because we do not consider improving low health literacy solely the duty of the patient, PHLI recognizes that health care professionals, too, play a key role in this initiative. As a company, we are interested in identifying methods to help improve health literacy, and in evaluating the impact of those tools.

To further develop this program, Pfizer sponsors four types of grants. Health Literacy Research grants are available to health care professionals and postgraduate investigators to develop two-year health literacy studies. Health Literacy Scholar awards are granted to professionals with doctorates (e.g. PhD, PharmD, EdD, MD) who undertake a health literacy research project. Visiting Lecturer grants are given to organizations to create a one-day lecture agenda suitable for a recognized health literacy expert. Health Literacy Community grants are provided to nonprofit organizations (e.g. community health centers, some hospitals) to produce community-based programs designed to increase health literacy in underserved populations. Our public health group also oversees a comprehensive health literacy study in 28 community health centers in Florida as part of Pfizer's Healthy State Initiative that is with the state's Medicaid program.

In addition to running its own grants and programs, Pfizer works in alliance with select public health associations and schools. We partner with organizations such as the American Public Health Association (APHA), the American College of Preventive Medicine (ACPM), the National Association of City and County Health Officers (NACCHO) and the Association of State and Territorial Health Officials (ASTHO) to improve the public health care community and to support prevention and public policy development. Additionally, we are embarking on a program with the Centers for Disease

Control and Prevention (CDC) to help attract physicians-in-training to the field of epidemiology by providing them access to CDC and state-based experience. Our partnership programs with various academic medical institutions encourage scholars to train in both infectious disease and clinical epidemiology.

The opportunities for someone in a position such as mine do not stop with programs and partnerships. When major national issues arise, I am there to act upon them. For example, one of my greatest challenges so far has resulted from the consequences of September 11, 2001, and the autumn anthrax attack. Because of my public health experience, I was designated the company's point person for these matters. We had to address such questions as: What should our company-wide response to bioterrorism be? Who are the right people on the outside to advise and help us? Did the CDC need us to produce more doxycycline for the pharmaceutical stockpile program? Did the Department of Defense (DoD), CDC or Food and Drug Administration (FDA) need our labs and/or manufacturing plants to increase product production?

Beyond my external activities, I play an internal role at Pfizer as well. In the case of the 9/11 disasters, my role has been to inform and educate employees about the issues and to keep them apprised of federal activities under way. Using my background in infectious diseases, medicine and epidemiology, I am able to address employee concerns. I continually assess our company's level of risk as a multinational corporation, no small task considering our headquarter offices are located between two high-profile structures, the United Nations and Grand Central Station.

This is an exciting time to be in public health and to be working within the private sector. I have an exceptional opportunity to transform the culture of an organization in the way it thinks about public health or in other words, to move towards a population focus. Although Pfizer is my home, practicing public health in any corporate setting is a wonderful opportunity to use your degree, your background and your public health experience to create change and add value to the public health community and to your company. Finding the right programs and the right strategic alliances that respond positively to both your business and to public health issues is a win-win proposition. And if the past is prologue, the bridges to be built between the private and public sectors will be increasingly important to the future of healthy populations.

Barbara A. DeBuono, MD, MPH, is Senior Medical Director and Group Leader for Public Health at Pfizer, having joined the company in September 2000. She received her undergraduate degree (1976) and medical degree (1980) from the University of Rochester and subsequently received a master's degree in Public Health from Harvard University in 1984.

Dr. DeBuono completed her medical internship and residency at the New England Deaconess Hospital in Boston, and then served as a Fellow in Infectious Diseases at Brown University Medical School's Affiliated Hospitals Program in Providence, Rhode Island, from 1984 through 1986. She is board certified in Internal Medicine and is a Fellow of the American College of Physicians. Dr. DeBuono served as Commissioner of Health for the State of New York in Governor George E. Pataki's cabinet from January 1995 through November 1998. Prior to coming to New York, Dr. DeBuono served as Rhode Island Department of Health State Epidemiologist from 1986 to 1991 and subsequently, Director of Health from 1991 to 1995. Dr. DeBuono has held academic appointments at Harvard as Clinical Instructor of Medicine, at Brown University Medical School as Associate Professor of Medicine and at the University at Albany, State University of New York as Professor of Health Policy. She currently holds the appointment of Clinical Professor of Medicine at Columbia University College of Physicians and Surgeons.

Dr. DeBuono has served on two IOM (Institute of Medicine) committees. She serves on the Advisory Committee to the Director of the Centers for Disease Control and Prevention. She is a member of the Board of the National Academy for State Health Policy and the Advisory Committee to the Health Care Financing Organization.

looking forward

By Hugh Tilson,
MD, DrPH,
Clinical
Professor of
Epidemiology
and Health
Policy, School
of Public
Health,
University of
North Carolina
at Chapel Hill,
Senior Advisor
to the Dean

The careers outlined in this book represent a small window into the enormous world of public health, where wonderful opportunities abound. The experts profiled here never cease to impress, amaze and inspire me, as I hope they do you. Many of them say their careers were determined as much by chance as by intent. Mine certainly has been! But I have always subscribed to the aphorism that serendipity favors the prepared mind. In fact, a theme that recurs in many of the chapters in this guide is how important it is to be prepared to face the multiple challenges of our field.

A second recurring theme is that the education of the past is but a preparation for the present and a forecast to the future, which is another way of saying that a career in public health is a career of lifetime learning. Consider what we did not know and how quickly we learned about infectious diseases

Hugh Tilson, MD, DrPH

such as HIV/AIDS, whose discovery and early responses have been detailed by Dr. James Curran. Or consider West Nile virus, discovered in New York State for the first time in 1999, which we read of in detail from Dr. Dale Morse. The international and global health chapter in this book describes the direct connection between iodine and a child's IQ and how providing sufficient iodine in a child's diet can alleviate potential problems. But learning and applying what we've learned do not always work in tandem. In her discussion of global HIV/AIDS, Dr. Helene Gayle points out the power of education, but explains how the work of health care providers is critical to giving prevention a fair chance.

The current public health climate is exhilarating in part because its challenges present so many fresh opportunities. Many of these challenges arose in the immediate aftermath of the terrorist attacks of 2001. Since then, the public has been troubled by the emergence of bioterrorist weapons, and public health issues have been thrust into the limelight. When legislators used the words "public health infrastructure" when they talked to the press about the solutions to our nation's lack of preparedness, many of this volume's contributors knew an important corner had been turned. The September 11 disaster also prompted national, state and local legislators to recognize the value of the public health systems in their states or municipalities. More and more they insist that these systems provide leadership, guidance and protection for their citizens. As these demands continue to evolve, public health agencies and organizations must raise funding to keep pace. The infrastructure proposals delineated throughout this book recognize the need for sustained federal appropriations and state and local contributions, to build and maintain public health resources.

Tip O'Neill, late Speaker of the U.S. House of Representatives from Cambridge, Massachusetts, once famously said, "All politics is local." My personal variant of that aphorism is "all public health begins at home." Locally, every community needs its own identifiable public health system, including health information databases with qualified personnel to run them. The informatics network is critical to a solid and effective infrastructure. Public health officials can no longer afford to learn about unfolding public health disasters and emergencies by watching cable news networks. What we know at the national level must immediately be available at the state and local levels, and that means instant bi-directional telecommunications — a database in every community's health department connecting directly to the state health department and the nation's public health nerve center, the Centers for Disease Control and Prevention (CDC) in Atlanta.

The workforce is an essential — perhaps the most essential — part of any infrastructure dependent on people. When considering what it will take to provide a workforce that delivers on the promises for the decade ahead, several matters become clear. First, as the population ages, public health services will expand and as they do, so will the number of jobs at all levels. Competitive salaries will be needed to keep public health careers on a level playing field with other occupations. Second, we need well-trained people with strong skills to fill those positions as they develop. Health professionals, including nurses, social workers, nutritionists, administrators, educators, pharmacists and physicians, should exhibit competencies not always provided by schools of public health or even public health certificate programs of the past. To this end, there is a movement afoot to consider developing separate public health credentials, parallel to what we see in our educational system. For example, someone wishing to teach biology can have a PhD in biology but still not be allowed in the classroom without a teacher's certificate. The same holds true in public health as well; an MD might not be well prepared for the public health challenges ahead. As you have read in Dr. Gebbie's chapter, a separate credentialing mechanism is being considered, designed to ensure that anyone who practices in public health demonstrates professional competence not only in his or her specialty, but also in the core essentials of public health.

A natural conceptual leap from credentialing for public health professionals is accreditation of community health agencies. The "National Public Health System Performance Standards," which were designed to evaluate the way communities deploy essential health services, have actually provided communities with a great opportunity for self-assessment. Might a national group such as the Joint Commission of Accreditation of Health Care Organizations (JCAHO) tweak these same standards to accredit communities, provided these communities demonstrate, through application of the public health system standards, that they are adequately protecting the health of the people?

Unacceptable disparities in health status among underserved subgroups of our population persist. For the infrastructure to work at maximum effectiveness to serve us all, and particularly to help us all address and overcome disparities, we need to capitalize on the potential for diversity in this profession. The positive lessons learned in the divisive '60s and '70s are that the workforce is stronger for its differences. Still, in this profession, many cultural and ethnic groups are underrepresented. We must make a strong effort to recruit a culturally balanced workforce to create an effective public health system. This principle especially applies to leadership positions. Leadership in the public health community must be developed from a large and culturally mixed pool of potential supervisors and directors, and that means involving and mentoring, in the integral workings of every facet of the profession, any qualified and promising people who request such assistance.

Two initiatives should be mentioned that I believe give us a preview of things to come in public health. The first, Public Health Grand Rounds, is a demonstration project jointly sponsored by the CDC and the University of North Carolina School of Public Health. In Public Health Grand Rounds, the "patient" is the community and the "condition" is a public health issue confronting the community, such as an epidemic, higher percentage of low-birth weight newborns or prevalent drug abuse.[1] The Grand Rounds team visits communities where a public health situation has occurred, interviews those who were involved in addressing it to learn the lessons they have learned, and creates a learning case study video. The video is then broadcast and web-cast live and nationwide from a studio at the CDC to thousands of viewers, who are generally in their local communities and watch the program

in groups. The world's leading experts on the subject critique the case, and viewers are encouraged to call in or fax their questions. The implications for the lifetime learner in public health of the future are exciting to think about.

The second initiative is the public health law program at the CDC, designed to improve the understanding of the interaction between law and public health and to strengthen the legal foundation for public health practice. There is a clear consensus that the archaic public health codes developed by every state over the past decades must be reviewed, aligned, and, as needed, refreshed in an on-going nationwide coordinated process.

Solutions to the public health challenges we face will be reached only if we choose to anticipate the problems of tomorrow. What sorts of problems? Antibiotic resistance, obesity and other epidemic chronic diseases, deterioration of our environment and barriers to medical care are some. Others we cannot always specify, such as the possibility of a major infectious disease emergence similar to the West Nile virus, or even the unpredictability of climate and weather, or disasters, natural or, tragically, man-made.

With a surveillance system properly tuned, a response system properly prepared and a support system regularly refreshed, we can face these challenges. These and other tools to address these situations will be available to you as never before. But in all our excitement about the future, let us not forget the enormous progress of preventive medicine over the past 50 years, which makes it possible for someone like myself — a guy in his 60s — to anticipate another 20 years of productive public health work. This opportunity for me and for a healthier America exists as a result of the insights,

leadership and resources of my contemporaries. But it's up to the next generation, those of you who are currently working toward degrees, to now step up to the helm. I'm personally looking forward to seeing you there.

Hugh Tilson, MD, DrPH is Clinical Professsor of Epidemiology and Health Policy at the School of Public Health at the University of North Carolina, where he serves as Senior Advisor to the Dean. A physician with his MD degree from Washington University in St. Louis, Missouri (1964), he is a Board Certified Specialist in Preventive Medicine and holds both a master's degree and doctoral degree in Public Health from the Harvard School of Public Health (1969–1972).

Dr. Tilson is a practicing epidemiologist and outcomes researcher, with a career in preventive medicine and public health spanning more than 30 years. Fifteen years of public service includes duties as a U.S. Army Preventive Medicine Officer in Europe; Consultant to the Federal Office of Economic Opportunity, National Center for Health Services Research, and Veterans Administration; Local Public Health Officer and Human Services Director for Portland, Oregon; and State Public Health Director for North Carolina. Before leaving Oregon for duties in North Carolina, he served as President of the National Association of County Health Officers. In June 1996, he joined the full-time faculty of the UNC School of Public Health.

Dr. Tilson currently serves on the Faculties of the North Carolina Schools of Medicine, Pharmacy and Public Health, where he is both Clinical and Adjunct Professor. He has served as chair of the Clinical Steering Committee for the Pharmaceutical Research and Manufacturers Association (PhRMA). A fellow of the American College of Epidemiology, and former Vice-chair of the American Board of Preventive Medicine, Dr. Tilson also served as President of the American College of Preventive Medicine from 1995 to 1997. A founding member of the American Academy of Pharmaceutical Physicians, he is AAPP Vice-President for Policy. Dr. Tilson is a liason to the Institute of Medicine Committee on Assuring the Health of the Public in the 21st Century.

1 http://www.publichealthgrandrounds.unc.edu

appendix

schools of public health

Boston University School
of Public Health
715 Albany Street
Boston, MA 02118
(617) 638-4640

Columbia University Mailman
School of Public Health
722 West 168th Street, 14th Floor
New York, NY 10032
(212) 305-3929

Emory University Rollins School
of Public Health
1518 Clifton Road N.E.
Atlanta, GA 30322
(404) 727-8720

George Washington University
School of Public Health Services
2300 Eye Street N.W.
Washington, DC 20037
(202) 994-5179

Harvard School of Public Health
677 Huntington Avenue
Boston, MA 02115
(617) 432-1025

Johns Hopkins Bloomberg School
of Public Health
615 North Wolfe Street
Baltimore, MD 21205-2179
(410) 955-3540

Loma Linda University School of
Public Health
Loma Linda, CA 92350
(909) 558-4578

Ohio State University School
of Public Health
College of Medicine and
Public Health
M-116 Starling Loving Hall
320 West 10th Avenue
Columbus, OH 43210-1240
(614) 293-3913

Saint Louis University School
of Public Health
3543 Lafayette Street, Suite 300
St. Louis, MO 63104-1314
(314) 977-8100

San Diego State University Graduate
School of Public Health
San Diego, CA 92182-4162
(619) 594-1255

Texas A&M School of Rural
Public Health
1266 TAMU
College Station, TX 77843-1266
(979) 845-2387

Tulane University School of Public
Health and Tropical Medicine
1440 Canal Street
New Orleans, LA 70112
(504) 588-5397

University at Albany SUNY School
of Public Health
One University Place
Rensselaer, NY 12144-3456
(518) 402-0283

University of Alabama at
Birmingham School of Public Health
1530 Third Avenue,
South RPHB 140
Birmingham, AL 35294-0022
(205) 975-7742

University of California at Berkeley
School of Public Health
19 Earl Warren Hall
Berkeley, CA 94720
(510) 643-0881

University of California at Los
Angeles School of Public Health
Center for the Health Sciences
P.O. Box 951772
Los Angeles, CA 90095
(310) 825-6381

University of Illinois at Chicago
School of Public Health
2121 West Taylor Street
Chicago, IL 60612
(312) 996-6620

University of Iowa College
of Public Health
2707 Steindler Building
Iowa City, IA 52242-1008
(319) 335-9833

University of Massachusetts School
of Public Health and Health Sciences
715 North Pleasant Street
108 Arnold House
Amherst, MA 01003-9304
(413) 545-1303

University of Medicine and
Dentistry of New Jersey-School
of Public Health
335 George Street
Liberty Plaza, Suite 2200
P.O. Box 2688
New Brunswick, NJ 08903-2688
(732) 235-9700

University of Michigan School
of Public Health
109 South Observatory Street
Ann Arbor, MI 48109-2029
(734) 763-5454

University of Minnesota School
of Public Health
Mayo Mail Code 197
420 Delaware Street S.E.
Minneapolis, MN 55455-0381
(612) 624-6669

University of North Carolina at
Chapel Hill School of Public Health
170 Rosenau Hall, CB #7400
Chapel Hill, NC 27599-7400
(919) 966-3215

University of North Texas
Health Science Center School
of Public Health
3500 Camp Bowie Boulevard
Fort Worth, TX 76107-2699
(817) 735-2252

University of Oklahoma College
of Public Health
P.O. Box 26901
801 NE 13th Street
Oklahoma City, OK 73104-5072
(405) 271-2232

University of Pittsburgh Graduate
School of Public Health
A-624 Crabtree Hall
130 De Soto Street
Pittsburgh, PA 15261
(412) 624-3001

University of Puerto Rico School
of Public Health
Medical Sciences Campus
P.O. Box 365067
San Juan, Puerto Rico 00936
(787) 764-5975

University of South Carolina,
The Norman J. Arnold School
of Public Health
800 Sumter Street
109 Health Sciences Building #76
Columbia, SC 29208
(803) 777-5032

University of South Florida college
of Public Health
13201 Bruce B. Downs Boulevard
(MDC-56)
Tampa, FL 33612-3805
(813) 974-6603

University of Texas School
of Public Health
P.O. Box 20186
Houston, TX 77225
(713) 500-9050

University of Washington
School of Public Health and
Community Medicine
P.O. Box 357230
Seattle, WA 98195
(206) 543-1144

Yale University School
of Public Health
School of Medicine
P.O. Box 208034
60 College Street
New Haven, CT 06520-8034
(203) 785-2867

public health programs

Arizona Graduate Program in Public
Health, Arizona State University,
Northern Arizona University and
University of Arizona
1501 North Campbell Avenue
P.O. Box 245163
Tucson, AZ 85724-5163
(520) 626-7083

Armstrong Atlantic State University
Department of Health Sciences
11935 Abercorn Street
Savannah, GA 31419-1997
(912) 927-5377

Bowling Green State University,
Medical College of Ohio,
University of Toledo
c/o Medical College of Ohio
Department of Public Health
4412 Collier Building
3015 Arlington Avenue
Toledo, OH 43614
(419) 383-4107

Brooklyn College, City University
of New York
Department of Health and
Nutrition Sciences
2900 Bedford Avenue
Brooklyn, NY 11210
(718) 951-5026

Brown University
Department of Community Health
P.O. Box 1860
Providence, RI 02912
(401) 863-3492

California State University, Fresno
Department of Health Science
College of Health and
Human Services
2345 East San Ramon Avenue
Fresno, CA 93740-0030

California State University,
Long Beach
College of Health & Human Services
1250 Bellflower Boulevard
Long Beach, CA 90840
(562) 985-4057

California State University,
Northridge
College of Health & Human
Development
18111 Nordhoff Street
Northridge, CA 91330
(818) 677-2997

Des Moines University-Osteopathic
Medical Center Public Health
Program
3200 Grand Avenue
Des Moines, IA 50312
(515) 271-1720

East Stroudsburg University
Health Department
East Stroudsburg, PA 18301
(570) 422-3560

East Tennessee State University
MPH Program
Department of Public Health
P.O. Box 70674
Johnson City, TN 37614-0674
(423) 439-4332

Eastern Virginia Medical
School/Old Dominion University
Graduate Program in Public Health
P.O. Box 1980
Norfolk, VA 23501-1980
(757) 446-6120

Florida A& M University
MPH Program
Institute of Public Health
Science Research Center,
Room 207D
Tallahassee, Florida 32307
(850) 599-3254

Florida International University
Graduate Program in Public Health
Department of Public Health
Biscayne Bay Campus
3000 Northeast 151st Street
North Miami, FL 33181-3600
(305) 919-5877

Hunter College, City University of
New York, MPH Program in Urban
Public Health
School of Health Sciences
CUNY, 425 East 25th Street
New York, NY 10010
(212) 481-5111

Indiana University at Bloomington
Department of Applied
Health Science
School of Health, Physical
Education and Recreation
Bloomington, IN 47405-4801
(812) 855-3627

Indiana University -Indianapolis
MPH Program
School of Medicine
Department of Public Health
1050 Wishard Boulevard, 4th Floor,
Room 4167
Indianapolis, IN 46202-2872
(317) 278-0337

Medical College of Wisconsin
Department of Preventive Medicine
8701 Watertown Plank Road
Milwaukee, WI 53226
(414) 456-4510

MPH Kansas Program, University of
Kansas, Wichita State University
Department of Preventive Medicine
1010 North Kansas
Wichita, KS 67214-3199
(316) 293-2627

Morehouse School of Medicine
MPH Program
Department of Community
Health & Preventive Medicine
720 Westview Drive S.W.
Atlanta, GA 30310-1495
(404) 752-1831

New Mexico State University
Department of Health Science
College of Health and Social Services
P.O. Box 30001, Department 3HLS
Las Cruces, NM 88003-8001
(505) 646-4300

New York University
Department of Health Studies
Steinhardt School of Education
35 West 4th Street, Suite 1200
New York, NY 10012
(212) 998-5780

Northern Illinois University
MPH Program
Public and Community
Health Programs
School of Allied Health Professions
DeKalb, IL 60115-2854
(815) 753-1384

Northwest Ohio Consortium MPH
of Public Health
c/o Medical College of Ohio
Department of Public Health
4412 Collier Building
3015 Arlington Avenue
Toledo, OH 43614
(419) 383-4107

Northwestern University
MPH Program
Feinberg School of Medicine
Department of Preventive Medicine
680 North Lake Shore Drive,
Suite 1102
Chicago, IL 60611
(312) 503-0027

Nova Southeastern University
MPH Program
College of Osteopathic Medicine
3200 South University Drive
Fort Lauderdale, FL 33328
(954) 262-1613

Oregon State University
Department of Public Health
319 Waldo Hall
Corvellis, OR 97331
(541) 738-3838

San Jose State University
Department of Health Science
School of Applied Sciences and Arts
San Jose, CA 95192
(408) 924-2970

Southern Connecticut State University
Department of Public Health
144 Farnham Avenue
New Haven, CT 06515-1355
(203) 392-6954

Temple University
Department of Health Studies
304 Vivacqua Hall
P.O. Box 2843
Philadelphia, PA 19122
(215) 204-8726

Tufts University School of Medicine
Graduate Programs in Public Health
Department of Family Medicine and
Community Health
136 Harrison Avenue
Boston, MA 02111
(617) 636-0935

Uniformed Services University of the
Health Sciences MPH, MTM&H,
MSPH Programs
Department of Preventive Medicine
and Biometrics
School of Medicine
4301 Jones Bridge Road
Bethesda, MD 20814-4799
(301) 295-3050

University of Colorado Health
Sciences Center
Department of Preventive Medicine
& Biometrics
School of Medicine, Health
Sciences Center
4200 East Ninth Avenue
P.O. Box C-245
Denver, CO 80262
(303) 315-8350

University of Connecticut Graduate
Program in Public Health
Department of Community
Medicine and Health Care
School of Medicine
Farmington, CT 06030-1910
(860) 679-3351

University of Hawaii MPH Program
John A. Burns School of Medicine
1960 East West Road
Honolulu, HI 96822
(808) 956-5739

University of Maryland, College Park
Department of Public and
Community Health
Valley Drive, Suite 2387
College Park, MD 20742-2611
(301) 405-2464

University of Miami MPH Program
Department of Epidemiology and
Public Health
P.O. Box 016069 (R669)
Miami, FL 33101
(305) 243-6759

University of New Mexico
MPH Program
School of Medicine
2400 Tucker N.E.
Albuquerque, NM 87131
(505) 272-4173

University of North Carolina,
Greensboro
Department of Public Health
Education
Health and Human Performance
Building, Suite 437
Greensboro, NC 27402-6169
(336) 334-5532

University of Northern Colorado
Department of Community Health
& Nutrition
College of Health & Human Sciences
Greeley, CO 80639
(970) 351-2755

University of Rochester
MPH Program
School of Medicine and Dentistry
601 Elmwood Avenue
P.O. Box 644
Rochester, NY 14642
(585) 275-7882

University of Southern California
MPH Program
Keck School of Medicine
Department of Preventive Medicine
1000 South Fremont Avenue,
Unit 8, Room 5133
Alhambra, CA 98103
(626) 457-6678

University of Southern Mississippi
MPH Program
Center for Community Health
College of Health & Human
Sciences
P.O. Box 5122
Hattiesburg, MS 39406-5122
(601) 266-5437

University of Tennessee, Knoxville
MPH Program
Department of Health &
Safety Sciences
College of Human Ecology
1914 Andy Holt Avenue
Knoxville, TN 37996-2710
(865) 974-6674

University of Texas Medical Branch
at Galveston Graduate Program in
Public Health
Department of Preventive Medicine
and Community Health
301 University Boulevard
1.116 Ewing Hall
Galveston, TX 77555-1150
(409) 772-1128

University of Utah
Department of Family and
Preventive Medicine
Public Health Programs
375 Chipeta Way, Suite A
Salt Lake City, UT 84108
(801) 587-3315

University of Wisconsin-La Crosse
Department of Health Education
and Health Promotion
203 Mitchell Hall
La Crosse, WI 54601
(608) 785-8163

Virginia Commonwealth University
Department of Preventive Medicine
and Community Health
P.O. Box 980212
Richmond, VA 23298-0212
(804) 828-9785

West Virginia University
Department of Community Medicine
Robert C. Byrd Health
Sciences Center
P.O. Box 9190
Morgantown, WV 26506-9190
(304) 293-2502

Western Kentucky University
Department of Public Health
1 Big Red Way
Bowling Green, KY 42101
(270) 745-4797

organizations and resources

Agency for Healthcare Research
and Quality (AHRQ)
2101 East Jefferson Street, Suite 501
Rockville, MD 20852
(301) 594-1364
Fax: (301) 594-2283

Agency for Toxic Substances and
Disease Registry (ATSDR)
1600 Clifton Road
Atlanta, GA 30333
(404) 498-0110
Fax: (404) 498-0057

American College of Preventive
Medicine (ACPM)
1307 New York Avenue N.W.,
Suite 200
Washington, DC 20005
(202) 466-2044
Fax: (202) 466-2662

The American Foundation for AIDS
Research (amfAR)
120 Wall Street, 13th Floor
New York, NY 10005-3902
(212) 806-1600
Fax: (212) 806-1601

American Medical Association
(AMA)
515 North State Street
Chicago, IL 60610
(312) 464-5000
Fax: (312) 464-4184

American Public Health Association
(APHA)
800 I Street N.W.
Washington, DC 20001-3710
(202) 777-APHA
Fax: (202) 777-2534

Association of Maternal and Child
Health Programs (AMCHP)
1220 19th Street N.W., Suite 801
Washington, DC 20036
(202) 775-0436
Fax: (202) 775-0061

Association of Public Health
Laboratories (APHL)
2025 M Street N.W., Suite 550
Washington, DC 20036
(202) 822-5227
Fax: (202)887-5098

Association of Schools of Public
Health (ASPH)
1101 15th Street N.W., Suite 910
Washington DC 20005
(202) 296-1099
Fax: (202) 296-1252

Association of State and Territorial
Health Officials (ASTHO)
1275 K. Street N.W., Suite 800
Washington, DC 20005-4006
(202) 391-9090
Fax: (212) 371-9797

Association of Teachers of
Preventive Medicine (ATPM)
1660 L Street N.W., Suite 208
Washington, DC 20036
(202) 463-0550
Fax: (202) 463-0555

Bill & Melinda Gates Foundation
P.O. Box 23350
Seattle, WA 98102
(206) 709-3400
Fax: (206) 709-3252

Centers for Disease Control and
Prevention (CDC)
1600 Clifton Road
Atlanta, GA 30333
(404) 639-3311

Children's Environmental Health
Network (CEHN)
110 Maryland Avenue N.E.,
Suite 511
Washington, DC 20002
(202) 543-4033
Fax: (202) 543-8797

Council on Education for Public
Health (CEPH)
800 I Street N.W., Suite 202
Washington, DC 20001-3710
(202) 789-1050
Fax: (202) 789-1895

Family Health International
P.O. Box 13950
Research Triangle Park, NC 27709
(919) 544-7040
Fax: (919) 544-7261

Health Resources and Services
Administration
U.S. Department of Health and
Human Services Parklawn Building
5600 Fishers Lane
Rockville, Maryland 20857
(301) 443-2403
Fax: (301) 443-1719

Indian Health Service
The Reyes Building
801 Thompson Avenue, Suite 400
Rockville, MD 20852-1627

Institute of Medicine (IOM)
500 Fifth Street N.W.
Washington, DC 20001
(202) 334-3300
Fax: (202) 334-3851

March of Dimes Birth Defects
Foundation
1275 Mamaroneck Avenue
White Plains, NY 10605
(914) 428-7100
Fax: (914) 997-4410

The National Alliance for
Hispanic Health
1501 Sixteenth Street N.W.
Washington, DC 20036
202-387-5000
Fax: (202) 797-4353

National Association of City
and County Health Officials
(NACCHO)
1100 17th Street, Second Floor
Washington, DC 20036
(202) 783-5550
Fax: (202) 783-1583

National Association of Community
Health Centers (NACHC)
7200 Wisconsin Avenue, Suite 210
Bethesda, MD 20814
(301) 347-0400
Fax: (301) 347-0459

National Association of Social
Workers (NASW)
750 First Street N.W.
Washington, DC 20002-4241
(202) 408-8600
Fax: (202) 336-8280

National Coalition of Hispanic
Health and Human Services
Organizations
1501 16th Street N.W.
Washington, DC 20036
(202) 387-5000
Fax: (202) 265-8027

National Healthy Start Association
P.O. Box 25227
Baltimore, MD 21229
(410) 525-1600
Fax: (410) 525-1601

National Institutes of Health (NIH)
900 Rockville Pike
Bethesda, MD 20892
(301) 496-4000

National Institute of Allergy and
Infectious Disease (NIAID)
Building 31, Room 7A-50
31 Center Drive MSC 2520
Bethesda, MD 20892-2520
(301) 496-5717

National Institute of Environmental
Health Sciences (NIEHS)
111 Alexander Drive
Research Triangle Park, NC 27709
(919) 541-3345

National Institute of Occupational
Safety and Health (NIOSH)
Robert A. Taft Laboratories
4676 Columbia Parkway
Cincinnati, OH 45226
(800) 356-4674
Fax: (513) 533-8573

National Mental Health Association
2001 North Beauregard Street,
12th Floor
Alexandria, VA 22311
(703) 684-7722
Fax: (703) 684-5968

National Public Health Leadership
Development Network
3545 Lafayette Avenue
St. Louis, MO 63104-1399
Fax: (314) 977-8150

National Public Health Leadership
Institute (NPHLI)
CB #8165
Chapel Hill, NC 27599-8165
(919) 843-7115
Fax: (919) 843-5563

National Student Nurses
Association (NSNA)
NSNA 45 Main Street, Suite 606
Brooklyn, NY 11201
(718) 210-0705
Fax: (718) 210-0710

Occupational Safety & Health
Administration (OSHA)
200 Constitution Avenue N.W.
Washington, DC 20210
(202) 693-2000
Fax: (202) 693-2106

Office of Minority Health
Rockwell II
5515 Security Lane, Suite 1000
Rockville, MD 20852
(301) 443-5084
Fax: (301) 594-0767

Public Health Foundation
1220 L Street N.W., Suite 350
Washington, DC 20005
(202) 898-5600
Fax: (202) 898-5609

Robert Wood Johnson Foundation
P.O. Box 2316
College Road East and Route 1
Princeton, NJ 08543-2316
(888) 631-9989
Fax: (609) 627-6401

Society for Nutrition Education
(SNE)
9202 North Meridian, Suite 200
Indianapolis, IN 46260
(800) 235-6690
Fax: (317) 571-5603

Society for Public Health Education
(SOPHE)
750 First Street N.E., Suite 910
Washington, DC 20002-4242
(202) 408-9804
Fax: (202) 408-9815

Substance Abuse and Mental Health
Services Administrations (SAMHSA)
5600 Fishers Lane
Rockville, MD 20857
(301) 443-0365
Fax: (301) 443-5447

UNAIDS
20, avenue Appia
CH-1211 Geneva 27
Switzerland
(+4122) 791 3666
Fax: (+4122) 791 4187

United Nations Children's Fund
(UNICEF)
3 United Nations Plaza
New York, New York 10017
(212) 326-7000
Fax: (212) 887-7465

U.S. Department of Health
and Human Services (U.S. Public
Health Service)
200 Independence Avenue S.W.
Washington, DC 20201
(202) 619-0257

World Health Organization (WHO)
Avenue Appia 20
1211 Geneva 27
Switzerland
(+00 41 22) 791 21 11
Fax: (+00 41 22) 791 3111

index

Henry Ford Health System, 77
HIV/AIDS, 8, 13-14, 94, 98, 150,
160-163
CDC's early intervention, 16-17
mother-to-child transmission
and, 162-163
partner notification and, 162
Hong Kong flu virus, 170
hospice care, 22
Human Genome Project, 149, 180

I

immunization, 16, 59
Indian Health Service (IHS),
8, 34, 207
informatics, 5, 180
Institute of Medicine (IOM), 9, 105,
147, 207
*"Assuring the Health of the
Public in the 21st Century"*
(report), 9

J

Jackson, Dick, federal environ-
mentalist, 117-123;
Career at a Glance, 123
Joint Commission of Accreditation
of Health Care Organizations
(JCAHO), 192

K

Kaiser Family Foundation,
94, 98, 101
Kellogg Foundation, The W. K., 27

L

laboratorian, 4, 139
lead concentration in children,
61, 120

Lednar, Wayne, corporate medical
director, 106-111;
Career at a Glance, 111
LeDuc, James, tropical disease
specialist, 165-170;
Career at a Glance, 170
Legionnaire's disease, 34, 117
Lewis, JoAnn, reproductive health
specialist, 153, 155-158;
Career at a Glance, 158
local public health professionals,
6, 14
Lyme disease, 117

M

Madigan Army Medical Center,
Tacoma, 106-107
malaria, 149
mammography, 15
Manson, JoAnn, research
epidemiologist, 37-42;
Career at a Glance, 42
March of Dimes Birth Defects
Foundation, 105, 207
Mary Washington College, 92
maternal and child health (MCH),
55-57
Medicaid/Medicare, 15, 23
Medicine/Public Health Initiative,
The, 79
meningococcal meningitis, 35, 130
mesothelioma (asbestos-related
cancer), 117
Morse, Dale, state epidemiologist,
129-134, 190; *Career at a
Glance,* 134
mortality in U.S., leading causes
of, 75